The Act of Will

AN ESALEN BOOK

The Esalen Publishing Program is edited by Stuart Miller

Also by Roberto Assagioli, M.D.

Psychosynthesis: A Manual of Principles and Techniques

The Act of Will

ROBERTO ASSAGIOLI, M.D.

The Viking Press : : New York

ACKNOWLEDGMENTS

Harper & Row, Publishers, Inc.:
From *Motivation and Personality* by Abraham Maslow.
From *Strength of Will and How to Develop It* by Boyd Barrett.

Oxford University Press:
From *A Confession, The Gospel in Brief, What I Believe* by Leo Tolstoi,
translated by Louise and Aylmer Maude and
published by Oxford University Press.

Presses Universitaires de France:
From *Caractère et personnalité* by Gaston Berger.

PREFACE

Everyone can have, or has had, the existential experience of "willing"—but often without full realization or a clear understanding. This book has been written as an introduction and a guide to such experience, and as a training manual. It is intended to be a tool for the exploration, development, and utilization of the will. It considers not only how the will *usually* operates, but how it can *best* operate. It describes the qualities of the will and its various aspects; the stages of the *willed act* and the purposes toward which this act can be directed. It is largely a phenomenological exploration based on my own experience and on statements and reports of my clients, students, and colleagues over many years. The amount of empirical data thus collected provides a sure ground for describing the various methods, techniques, and exercises for the practical training of the will and for its optimum use at all levels of existence—from the personal to the transpersonal and reaching into the realm where the individual will merges with the universal will.

This volume is also a preliminary map of the act of willing from the point of view of the newer developments in psychology—that is to say, existential, humanistic, and transpersonal psychology—although it has roots in various older contributions.

Because the subject is so challenging, I have made the style as simple as possible. But on occasion this simplicity is deceptive. I suggest that not only can this volume be read as a piece of interesting information but that it can profitably be studied in depth, and the many techniques practiced and applied in daily life. The chapters on Love and Will, the Transpersonal Will, and the Universal Will might bear particular consideration, as their subjects may be new to many readers. I should also like to mention that certain repetitions are deliberate and are intended for emphasis, and that cross-references in various parts of the text may help one to grasp both the manifold nature of the subject and its underlying unity.

As for language, the reader will find the word "will" used as a noun throughout. This has been done for the purpose of simplifying the text. However, it should be noted at the outset that no "metaphysical" claim is being made either for or against the proposition that the "will" exists. My approach, dealing as it does with "willers" and "willed acts," is empirical and phenomenological. Its foundation is psychosynthesis, both personal and transpersonal: a process of growth based on the harmonious integration of all aspects of the personality around the self, the center of awareness and will. So this book can take its place as a sequel to my previous one, *Psychosynthesis*,* in which the subject of the will was briefly introduced.

* An Esalen Book, New York: Viking/Compass, 1971.

I hope and trust that it may be a useful companion to many who want to develop and make good use of their wills. Much remains to be done, and toward this end I suggest in the *Will Project* (Part Three) a general plan both for individuals and for groups to continue the work of study and research. Such a plan is greatly needed at present because of the unfortunate neglect or misuse of the will and because of the enormous potential inherent in its right use for achieving self-actualization and Self-realization, and for solving major human problems.

Now I want to express my gratitude to all who have assisted in the production of the book. First, to my many students, clients, and co-workers who read portions of the manuscript at various times, offered their comments and suggestions, and helped generally. Of this large group, I would like to single out for particular mention Stuart Miller, editor of the Esalen/Viking series, whose many perceptive comments, suggestions, and additions were deeply appreciated; James Vargiu, who studied the manuscript in depth, making valuable suggestions and adding examples; and Susan Vargiu who greatly helped in this work by reordering the original text. Others to whom I gladly recognize my indebtedness are Dr. Frank Haronian, Betsie Carter, Steven Kull, and Dr. Piero Ferrucci. Ida Palombi, Vice-President of the Istituto di Psicosintesi in Florence, and my friend Kenneth Leslie-Smith also gave valuable cooperation.

With good will and the trust that the development of the will may have a substantial role in the emergence of a new period of human cooperation, I leave the next steps to the reader.

Florence, Italy
September, 1972

CONTENTS

Part One
The Nature of the Will

1

INTRODUCTION

If a man from a previous civilization—an ancient Greek, let us say, or a Roman—suddenly appeared among present-day humanity, his first impressions would probably lead him to regard it as a race of magicians and demigods. But were he a Plato or a Marcus Aurelius and refused to be dazzled by the material wonders created by advanced technology, and were he to examine the human condition more carefully, his first impressions would give place to great dismay.

He would soon notice that, though man has acquired an impressive degree of power over nature, his knowledge of and control over his inner being is very limited. He would perceive that this modern "magician," capable of descending to the bottom of the ocean and projecting himself to the moon, is largely ignorant of what is going on in the depths of his unconscious and is unable to reach up to the luminous superconscious levels, and to become aware of his true Self. This supposed demigod, controlling great electrical forces with a movement of the finger and flooding the air with sound and pictures for the entertainment of millions, would be seen to be incapable of dealing with his own emotions, impulses, and desires.

As several writers, Toynbee among them, have pointed out, this wide gulf between man's external and inner powers is one of the most important and profound causes of the individual and collective evils which afflict our civilization and gravely menace its future. Man has had to pay dearly for his material achievements. His life has become richer, broader, and more stimulating, but at the same time more complicated and exhausting. Its rapidly increasing tempo, the opportunities it offers for gratifying his desires, and the intricate economic and social machinery in which it has enmeshed him make ever more insistent demands on his energy, his mental functions, his emotions, and his will. For convincing evidence of this it would suffice to observe the day of the average businessman or politician, or career woman or housewife.

The individual often lacks the resources to cope with the difficulties and pitfalls of this kind of existence. His resistance may crumble in the face of the demands, the confusions, and the enticements it imposes. The ensuing disturbance leads to increasing discouragement and frustration—even to desperation.

The remedy for these evils—the narrowing and eventual closing of the fatal gap between man's external and his inner powers—has been and should be sought in two directions: *the simplification of his inner life,* and *the development of his inner powers.* Let us examine in what ways and to what extent these two procedures can provide the needed remedies.

The Simplification of the External Life

The trend toward simplicity began even before the rise

and expansion of modern technology as a reaction against the increasing complications and artificialities of "civilized" life. Its greatest exponents have been Jean-Jacques Rousseau, with his appeal for a return to nature, and Thoreau, who renounced the benefits of civilization and withdrew to lead the solitary "simple life" which he described so ably in *Walden*. Recently, disillusionment with the "blessings" of technological achievement has exploded into extreme and increasingly bitter indictments of the whole structure of modern civilization, into a wholesale rejection of our present "way of life."

Up to a certain point, the simplification of life is feasible and desirable. To some extent everyone is able to resist the attractions of the world and the pace of modern life, eliminate many unnecessary complications, re-establish closer contact with nature, and practice the art of relaxing and resting at intervals. But past a certain point, one encounters great difficulties. Duties of every kind, family ties, professional obligations keep us bound to the wheel of modern life and often compel us to conform to its hurried pace.

But even if circumstances permitted a very high degree of simplification and it were put into practice, the problem would be only partially solved. Modern man certainly could not—nor indeed has he reason to—abdicate from the predominant position, and the consequent responsibility, he has acquired on this planet. The evil does not lie in the technological powers themselves but in the *uses* to which man puts them and in the fact that he has allowed them to overwhelm and enslave him. Resistance to the prevailing negative trends of modern life calls for much determination, much firmness and persistence, much clear-sightedness and wisdom. But these are precisely the *inner* qualities and powers in which modern man is sorely lacking. So we are led to the necessity of recourse to the second procedure.

The Development of Man's Inner Powers

Only the development of his inner powers can offset the dangers inherent in man's losing control of the tremendous natural forces at his disposal and becoming the victim of his own achievements. A vivid realization that this is indispensable for maintaining the sanity and indeed the very survival of humanity, that only thus can man fulfill his true nature, should spur him on to tackle this task with an intensity of desire and determination equal to that which he has previously devoted to his external attainments.

Fundamental among these inner powers, and the one to which priority should be given, is the tremendous, unrealized potency of man's own *will.* Its training and use constitute the foundation of all endeavors. There are two reasons for this: the first is the will's central position in man's personality and its intimate connection with the core of his being—his very self. The second lies in the will's function in deciding what is to be done, in applying all the necessary means for its realization and in persisting in the task in the face of all obstacles and difficulties.

But when one decides to start this task, one is apt to be confused and baffled. A historical survey of the problems related to the will shows that attempts to solve this problem on theoretical, intellectualistic lines lead not only to no solution, but to contradiction, confusion, and bewilderment (see Appendix Four, pages 235ff.).

Therefore I believe that the right procedure is to postpone all intellectual discussions and theories on the subject, and begin by *discovering* the reality and the nature of the will *through its direct existential experience.*

2

THE EXISTENTIAL
EXPERIENCE OF THE WILL

The experience of the will constitutes both a firm foundation and a strong incentive for starting the exacting but most rewarding task of its training. It occurs in three phases: the first is the recognition that *the will exists*; the second concerns the realization of *having a will*. The third phase of the discovery, which renders it complete and effective, is that of *being a will* (this is different from "having" a will).

This discovery of the will is hard to describe; as is true of any experience, it cannot be fully communicated by words, but the paths leading to it and the conditions favoring it can be indicated. An analogy to the discovery of beauty, to the arousal of the aesthetic sense, may be illuminating: A revelation occurs, an "awakening" which may come when one looks at the delicate hue of the sky at sunset, at a majestic range of snow-capped mountains, or into the clear eyes of a child. It may come while contemplating the cryptic smile of Leonardo's "Gioconda." It may come while listening to the music of Bach or Beethoven, or while reading the inspired verses of great poets.

This awakened sense of the beautiful, though often faint and confused at first, becomes clearer and develops through repeated experiences of an aesthetic nature, and can also be cultivated and refined through the study of aesthetics and the history of art. But no amount of intellectual consideration and study can of itself take the place of the initial revelation.

The awakening can be facilitated and often brought about by creating favorable circumstances for this purpose; for instance, by the quiet and repeated contemplation of natural scenery and works of art, or by opening oneself to the charm of music.

The same is true of the will. At a given moment, perhaps during a crisis, one has a vivid and unmistakable inner experience of its reality and nature. When danger threatens to paralyze us, suddenly, from the mysterious depths of our being, surges an unsuspected strength which enables us to place a firm foot on the edge of the precipice or confront an aggressor calmly and resolutely. Before the threatening attitude of an unfair superior or when facing an excited mob, when personal reasons would induce us to yield, the will gives us the power to say resolutely: "No! At all costs I stand by my convictions; I will perform what I take to be right." Similarly, when assailed by some insinuating and seducing temptation, the will raises us, shaking us out of our acquiescence and freeing us from the snare.

The inner experience of "willing" may come also in other, more quiet and subtle ways. During periods of silence and meditation, in the careful examination of our motives, in moments of thoughtful deliberation and decision, a "voice," small but distinct, will sometimes make itself heard urging us to a specific course of action, a prompting which is different from that of our ordinary motives and impulses. We feel that it comes from the central core of our being. Or else an inner illumination makes us aware of the *reality* of the will with an overwhelming conviction that asserts itself irresistibly.

However, the simplest and most frequent way in which we discover our will is through determined action and struggle. When we make a physical or mental effort, when we are actively wrestling with some obstacle or coping with opposing forces, we feel a specific power rising up within us; and this inner energy gives us the experience of "willing."

Let us realize thoroughly the full meaning and immense value of the discovery of the will. In whatever way it happens, either spontaneously or through conscious action, in a crisis or in the quiet of inner recollection, it constitutes a most important and decisive event in our lives.

The discovery of the will in oneself, and even more the realization that the self and the will are intimately connected, may come as a real revelation which can change, often radically, a man's self-awareness and his whole attitude toward himself, other people, and the world. He perceives that he is a "living subject" endowed with the power to choose, to relate, to bring about changes in his own personality, in others, in circumstances. This enhanced awareness, this "awakening" and vision of new, unlimited potentialities for inner expansion and outer action, gives a new feeling of confidence, security, joy—a sense of "wholeness."

But this initial revelation, this inner light, however vivid and inspiring at the moment of its occurrence, is apt to grow dim and to flicker out or give only intermittent flashes. The new awareness of self and will becomes easily submerged by the constant surge of drives, desires, emotions, and ideas. It is crowded out by the ceaseless inrush of impressions from the outer world. Thus the need to protect, cultivate, and strengthen the initial attainment becomes evident, in order to make it a constant possession and utilize its great possibilities.

But when one puts oneself to this task, one finds oneself confronted by difficulties, and experiencing resistance. The first resistance is often due to the current misunderstanding about the nature and function of the will. The Victorian conception of the will still prevails, a conception of something stern and forbidding, which condemns and represses most of the other aspects of human nature. But such a misconception might be called a caricature of the will. The true function of the will is not to act against the personality drives to *force* the accomplishment of one's purposes. The will has a *directive* and *regulatory* function; it balances and constructively utilizes all the other activities and energies of the human being without repressing any of them.

The function of the will is similar to that performed by the helmsman of a ship. He knows what the ship's course should be, and keeps her steadily on it, despite the drifts caused by the wind and current. But the power he needs to turn the wheel is altogether different from that required to propel the ship through the water, whether it be generated by engines, the pressure of the winds on the sail, or the efforts of rowers.

Another form of resistance comes from the generally prevailing tendency toward inertia, to let the "easygoing" side of one's nature take control, to allow inner impulses or external influences to dominate the personality. It may be summed up as unwillingness to "take the trouble," to pay the price demanded by a worth-while undertaking. This often holds true for the development of the will; but it cannot reasonably be expected that the training of the will can be accomplished without the expenditure of effort and persistence required for the successful development of any other quality, whether physical or mental. And such effort is more than worth while, because the use of the will is at the basis of every activity. Therefore a more developed will improves the effectiveness of all future endeavors.

After the conviction, the certainty, that the will exists, and that one has a will, is acquired, comes the realization of the close, intimate connection between the will and the self. This culminates in the existential experience of pure self-consciousness, the direct awareness of the self, the discovery of the "I." In reality, this experience is implicit in our human consciousness. It is that which distinguishes it from that of animals, which are conscious but not self-conscious. Animals are conscious: they clearly show this in their emotional reactions to situations and their effective relations with human beings. Human beings go beyond mere animal awareness and *know that they are aware*. But generally this self-consciousness is indeed implicit rather than explicit. It is experienced in a rather nebulous and distorted way because it is usually mixed with, and veiled by, the contents of consciousness (sensations, drives, emotions, thoughts, etc.). Their constant impact veils the clarity of consciousness and produces spurious identification of the self with these changing and transient contents. Thus, if we are to make self-consciousness explicit, clear, and vivid, we must disidentify ourselves from all these contents and *identify with the self.* It is possible to achieve this realization by means of certain kinds of meditation, but particularly by the use of the Exercise of Self-Identification, which is given in my book *Psychosynthesis* and quoted here in Appendix One (page 211) for the convenience of the reader.

Self-consciousness, or awareness of the self, has two characteristics: one *introspective,* the other *dynamic.* This can be expressed in various ways: for instance, "I am aware of being and willing"; or "In that I am, I can will." This intimate relationship between the "I" and the will, between being and willing, has been clearly set forth by Professor Calò in his article on the will in the *Italian Encyclopedia*:

> Volitional activity is in close connection with the conscious-ness of the *I* as both an active and a unifying center of all the elements of psychic life. The *I*, which is at first an obscure subjectivity, a point of reference of every psychic experience, affirms itself gradually as it succeeds in distinguishing itself, as a source of activity, from every one of its particular elements (feelings, tendencies, instincts, ideas). The will is just this activity of the *I* which is a unity, which stands above the multiplicity of its contents, and which replaces the previous impulsive, fractional, centrifugal action of those contents. *I* and *will* are correlated terms; the *I* exists in so far as it has its own specific capacity for action which is the will; and the will exists only as a distinctive and autonomous activity of the *I*.*

It is well to become aware of the relationships between the self and the will on one hand and the various other psychological functions on the other. This awareness may be clarified by the diagram on page 13.

The will has been placed at the center of the diagram in direct contact with the conscious *I*, or personal self, to show the close connection between them. *Through* the will, the *I* acts on the other psychological functions,

* Reference notes begin on page 263.

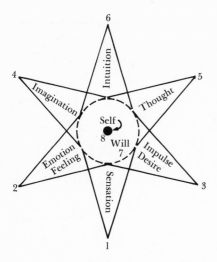

1. Sensation
2. Emotion — Feeling
3. Impulse — Desire
4. Imagination
5. Thought
6. Intuition
7. Will
8. Central point:
   The I, or personal self

regulating and directing them. The diagram is oversimplified, like all diagrams, but it helps to give prominence to the central position of the will.

But there remains a further step that can be taken, a further discovery that can be made—that of the relationship between the *I* and the Transpersonal, or higher, Self, of which the *I* is a reflection or projection. This relationship is depicted in the diagram on page 14 of the psychological constitution of man.

The *I* is indicated by the point at the center of the field of awareness, while the Transpersonal Self is represented by a star at the apex of the superconscious. I will not dwell further on this here, because the subject is dealt with in the chapter on the Transpersonal Will, which is a function of the Transpersonal Self.

To begin the discussion of the training of the will

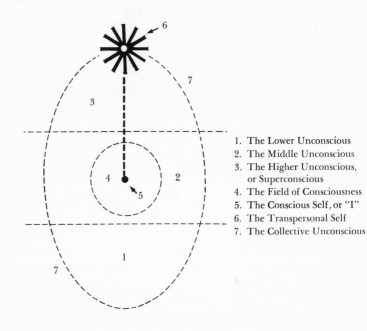

1. The Lower Unconscious
2. The Middle Unconscious
3. The Higher Unconscious,
   or Superconscious
4. The Field of Consciousness
5. The Conscious Self, or "I"
6. The Transpersonal Self
7. The Collective Unconscious

requires laying some conceptual groundwork. Because of the richness of the subject, I hope the reader will bear with me in the elaboration of categories in describing the will. These categories are necessary to get a complete picture of the fully developed will and, most important, to get a purchase on training such an important human attribute.

I shall use three categories—or dimensions—in describing the will: aspects, qualities, and stages. The first category, *aspects,* is the most basic, and represents the *facets* that can be recognized in the fully developed will. The second category, *qualities,* refers to the expression of the will: these are the *modes of expression* of the will-in-action. Finally, the *stages* of the will refer specifically to the *process* of willing, the act of will as it unfolds from beginning to end.

The fully developed will can be thought of as having a number of different major *aspects;* these should be thought of as the principal facets of our main subject, the *major* elements in the outline of the will. Each of these aspects can be trained in specific and appropriate ways. Because the bulk of Part One of this volume is concerned with these major aspects, it is well to outline them at once. The aspects of the fully developed human will are the *strong will,* the *skillful will,* the *good will,* and the *Transpersonal Will.* Let me describe these principal aspects of the will briefly so that the reader can have them in mind as we continue to outline the phenomenology of the will in other regards.

1. *The Strong Will.* As we have previously mentioned, to train the will one must start by *recognizing* that the will exists; then that one *has* a will; and finally that one *is* a will, or, essentially, a "willing self." Then one has to *develop* the will and make it strong enough to be adequate for its manifold uses in all the domains of life. Most misunderstandings and mistakes concerning the will arise from the frequent misconception that the strong will constitutes the whole will. Strength is *only one* of the aspects of the will, and when dissociated from the others, it can be, and often is, ineffectual or harmful to oneself and other people.

2. *The Skillful Will.* The skillful aspect of the will consists of the ability to obtain desired results with the least possible expenditure of energy. In order to go somewhere, one does not proceed by walking in a straight line across open country or by climbing over buildings. One rather studies a road map and uses existing roads, which, although not in a straight line, can lead one to his destination with the least amount of effort. And one takes advantage of already existing means of transportation,

that is, of vehicles that are going in the direction he has chosen.

Similarly, in order to use our will most skillfully, we need to understand our inner constitution, become acquainted with our many different functions, drives, desires, habit patterns, and the relationships between them, so that at any one time we can activate and utilize those aspects of ourselves that already have the tendency to produce the specific action or condition we are aiming for.

3. *The Good Will.* Even when the will is endowed with both strength and skill, it is not always satisfactory. In fact, it may even be a very harmful weapon, for if such a will is directed toward evil ends, it becomes a serious danger to society. A man of strong and able will, capable of using his natural gifts to the utmost, can overpower or corrupt the will of others; one who dares everything, fears nothing, and whose actions are not restrained by any ethical consideration, by any sense of love or compassion, can have a disastrous influence on a community or even an entire nation.

There are two great laws which operate in the physical and in the psychological worlds: the *Law of action and reaction,* and the *Law of rhythm and equilibrium.* Through their operation, those who cause harm attract harm upon themselves; those who are violent and merciless ultimately evoke the violence and cruelty of others against themselves. History offers many such examples, from Caligula to Rasputin to Hitler. Because of the working of these laws, the will, to be fulfilling, must be *good.* Thus, good will is both desirable and ultimately inevitable. It may therefore be stated that learning to choose *right* goals is an essential aspect of training of the will. It is necessary, both for the general welfare and for our own, that our will be *good* as well as strong and skillful. All this is the specific field of interpersonal, group, and social psychosynthesis.

4. *The Transpersonal Will.* The three aspects of the will so far mentioned seem to constitute the totality of the characteristics of the will. This may be true for the "normal" human being, in whom they suffice for his self-actualization and for leading a rich and useful life. This represents the aim of *personal* and *interpersonal* psychosynthesis. But there is another dimension in man. Though many are unaware of it and may even deny its existence, there is another kind of awareness, to the reality of which the direct experience of a number of individuals has testified throughout history. The dimension along which this awareness functions can be termed "vertical." In the past, it was generally considered the domain of religious, or "spiritual," experience, but it is now gaining increasing recognition as a valid field of scientific investigation.

This is the specific domain of transpersonal psychology, which deals with what Maslow, a pioneer in the field, has called the "higher needs." In the words of the "Statement of Purpose" of the *Journal of Transpersonal Psychology* its concern is with: "metaneeds, ultimate values, unitive consciousness, peak experiences, ecstasy, mystical experience, B[eing] values, essence, bliss, awe, wonder, self-actualization, ultimate meaning, transcendence of the self, spirit, sacralization of everyday life, oneness, cosmic awareness, cosmic play, individual and species-wide synergy, maximal interpersonal encounter, transcendental phenomena, maximal sensory awareness, responsiveness and expression; and related concepts, experiences, and activities."

This is the realm or dimension of the Transpersonal

Will, which is *the will of the Transpersonal Self.* It is also the field of the relationship within each individual between the will of the personal self or *I,* and the will of the Transpersonal Self. This relationship leads to a growing interplay between, and ultimately to the fusion of, the personal and transpersonal selves and in turn to their relationship with the ultimate reality, the Universal Self, which embodies and demonstrates the Universal, Transcendent Will.

3

THE QUALITIES OF
THE WILL

Before we embark on a detailed examination of the four
major aspects of the will and how they can be developed
by training, it will be useful to review the *qualities* of the
will. If we study the phenomenology of the will-in-action,
that is, the characteristics displayed by willers, we find a
number of *qualities* which are outstanding in the great
willers, and which exist also in some measure, however
small, in each of us and, if necessary, can be aroused from
latency to manifestation. These qualities are likely to be
more familiar to most readers than the aspects. The
qualities of the will are:

1. Energy—Dynamic Power—Intensity
2. Mastery—Control—Discipline
3. Concentration—One-Pointedness—Attention—
Focus
4. Determination—Decisiveness—Resoluteness—
Promptness
5. Persistence—Endurance—Patience
6. Initiative—Courage—Daring
7. Organization—Integration—Synthesis

From the standpoint of training the will it is necessary first to have the various qualities clearly in view; to know them and understand them thoroughly. Then they can be evoked as necessary in the right proportions and in the proper mode as the situation demands. Different qualities are more closely associated with specific aspects and stages of the will,* and we shall discuss these concurrences as we proceed. It should also be remembered that some of the qualities are closely related to each other and overlap to some extent. Such is the case, for example, with the qualities of Mastery, Concentration, Decisiveness, and Initiative. Other qualities, instead, have opposite characteristics. The fully developed will knows how to use these differing qualities alternately, as needed, or to achieve a balance between them by following a wise middle path. Sometimes, for example, the best completion of a willed act calls for the balancing of Decisiveness and Daring on one hand, and Discipline and Persistence on the other.

1. Energy—Dynamic Power—Intensity

This quality is the naturally outstanding characteristic of the *strong will*. It is the one quality which is generally attributed to the will and with which the will is often identified. But it is not the only quality of the will, and if it is not associated with other qualities and balanced by the action of other psychological functions, it is apt to defeat its own purposes. This quality, taken by itself, can have harmful and even disastrous effects on both the willer himself and on the targets of his "willful" actions.

---

* The stages of the willed act, as it unfolds from start to finish, are: Purpose, Deliberation, Decision, Affirmation, Planning, and the Direction of the Execution. The full discussion of these stages is Part Two of this volume.

Such effects occur when the will is used in a domineering, oppressive, forbidding way; it has been called the "Victorian" will, because it was widely used in that period, particularly in the field of education. It is such misuse that has brought the will into disrepute, producing a violent reaction against it which has swung to the other extreme: a tendency to refuse any kind of control and discipline of drives, urges, wishes, whims—a cult of unbridled "spontaneity."

Thus, a proper understanding of the will includes a clear and balanced view of its dual nature: two different but not contradictory poles. On one hand the "power element" needs to be recognized, appreciated, if necessary strengthened, and then wisely applied. At the same time it must be recognized that there are volitional acts which do not necessarily require effort. On the basis of experimental research, Aveling and others have observed that "a volition ensuing even in difficult action may be absolutely effortless. . . ."

It can be said that particularly the stages of intention, evaluation, and choice can be effortless. Moreover, there is another and higher condition in which the personal will is effortless; it occurs when the willer is so identified with the Transpersonal Will, or, at a still higher and more inclusive level, with the Universal Will, that his activities are accomplished with free spontaneity, a state in which he feels himself to be a willing channel into and through which powerful energies flow and operate. This is *wu-wei*, or the "taoistic state," mentioned by Maslow in *The Farther Reaches of Human Nature*.

Understanding the existence of the two "poles" of the will, one can deal without resistances or misunderstandings with its "power" element. This is a direct, existential experience which, as previously mentioned, is realized when there is conflict or effort due to opposing conditions or forces that one wills to overcome. One is then clearly aware of, he can feel, the measure of *intensity* of the will needed for overcoming opposing forces. This is analogous to, and is felt in the same direct way as, the way an athlete feels the degree of muscular effort that he must make in order to jump above a high obstacle.

2. Mastery—Control—Discipline

This quality of the will is closely connected with the first, both because mastery and control require energy and effort and because one of the chief uses of the energy of the will is to exercise control over the other psychological functions. Control and discipline are qualities which, at present, often arouse diffidence and antagonism. Again, this is due to an extreme reaction against their previously excessive and mistaken enforcement. Control does *not* mean repression or suppression. Repression implies unconscious condemnation or fear (or both!) and the consequent endeavor to prevent the repressed material from emerging from the unconscious to consciousness. Suppression is the conscious and forceful elimination of unwanted material from our awareness, thus preventing its expression. Right control, however, means the *regulation of expression,* aiming at a guided, constructive utilization of the biological and psychological energies. Thus in practice wise control is often quite the opposite of repression and suppression.

The same can be said of *inhibition.* Here again, the antagonism aroused by this word is due to a misunderstanding of its real meaning and function. Inhibition is *not* suppression; it is a *temporary* check of reflex actions. This is clearly recognized in the field of neurophysiology. Immediate response to stimulation is a function of the nervous centers in the spine, while one of the chief functions of the brain is that of inhibiting such reactions temporarily. This enables the stimulus to propagate to other areas of the brain, where it creates associations, often manifold and complex, which in turn make possible a higher kind of response—intelligent, well adapted, and useful. This applies not only to physiological responses, but also to psychological actions. The point has been well stated by Maslow:

> An easy mistake here is to think of spontaneity and expressiveness as good always, and control of any kind as bad and undesirable. This is not so . . . there are several meanings of self-control, or of inhibition, and some of them are quite desirable and healthy, even apart from what is necessary for dealing with the outside world. Control need not mean frustration or renunciation of basic need gratifications. What I would call the "Apollonizing controls" do *not* call the gratification of needs into question at all; they make them *more* rather than less enjoyable by e.g. suitable delay (as in sex), by gracefulness (as in dancing or swimming), by estheticizing (as with food and drink), by stylizing (as in sonnets), by ceremonializing, sacralizing, dignifying, by doing something well rather than just doing it.

> And then too, what has to be repeated again and again is that the healthy person is not only expressive. He must be able to be expressive when he wishes to be. He must be able to let himself go. He must be able to drop controls, inhibitions, defenses when he deems this desirable. But equally, he must have the ability to control himself, to delay his pleasures, to be polite to avoid hurting, to keep his mouth shut, and to rein his impulses. He must be able to be either Dionysian or Apollonian, Stoic or Epicurean, expressive or coping, controlled or uncontrolled, self-disclosing or self-concealing, able to have fun and able to give up fun, able to think of the future as well as the present. The healthy or self-actualizing person is essentially

versatile; he has lost fewer of the human capabilities than the average man has. He has a larger armamentarium of responses and moves toward full humanness as a limit; that is, he has *all* the human capacities.

Control and discipline are needed in all kinds of training, both in learning necessary skills and techniques and in actualizing the unlimited amount of human potential. This means first developing weak psychological functions to a normal level, and then bringing normal capacities to a higher degree of effectiveness. The point is obvious and is more or less consciously accepted and taken for granted in all forms of sport and also in the development of the technical skills necessary for artistic expression. The recognition and acceptance of the need for discipline has been expressed by a great violinist—Kubelik, I believe: "If I don't practice for a day, I am aware of the difference; if I don't practice for two days, my friends notice it; if I don't practice for three days the public remarks on it." The use of control and discipline is of course basic also in the training of the will itself, as will be clear in later chapters.

The result of all control, discipline, and training is the achievement of *mastery,* which gives us both maximum effectiveness and the most intense and enduring sense of assurance, satisfaction, and joy.

3. Concentration—One-Pointedness—Attention—
   Focus

This is an essential quality of the will. The lack of it can render even a strong will ineffectual, while its application may successfully compensate for a relative weakness in the force or "voltage" of the will. Its action is analogous to that of a lens, which by focusing the rays of the sun concentrates and intensifies the heat.

Concentration is produced by attention, the function of which in the act of the will has been well emphasized by William James. Such attention can be "involuntary," in the sense that it can be produced by a need or prevailing interest. But when the object of the attention is not attractive or "interesting" in itself, attention requires one-pointed concentration and sustained effort.

An interesting anecdote illustrating the point is told by Ramacharaka in his book *Raja Yoga*. He speaks of the famous naturalist Agassiz and his method of training pupils:

> His pupils became renowned for their close powers of observation and perception, and their consequent ability to "think" about the things they had seen. Many of them rose to eminent positions, and claimed that this was largely by reason of their careful training.
>
> The tale runs that a new student presented himself to Agassiz one day, asking to be set to work. The naturalist took a fish from a jar in which it had been preserved, and laying it before the young student, bade him observe it carefully, and be ready to report upon what he had noticed about the fish. The student was then left alone with the fish. There was nothing especially interesting about that fish—it was like many other fishes that he had seen before. He noticed that it had fins and scales, and a mouth and eyes, yes, and a tail. In a half-hour he felt certain that he had observed all about the fish that there was to be perceived. But the naturalist remained away.
>
> The time rolled on, and the youth, having nothing else to do, began to grow restless and weary. He started out to hunt up the teacher, but he failed to find him, and so had to return and gaze again at that wearisome fish. Several hours had passed, and he knew but little more about the fish than he did in the first place.
>
> He went out to lunch, and when he returned it was still a case of watching the fish. He felt disgusted and discouraged,

and wished he had never come to Agassiz, who, it seemed, was a stupid old man after all—one way behind the times. Then, in order to kill time, he began to count the scales. This completed, he counted the spines of the fins. Then he began to draw a picture of the fish. In drawing the picture he noticed that the fish had no eyelids. He thus made the discovery that as his teacher had expressed it often, in lectures, "a pencil is the best of eyes." Shortly after the teacher returned, and after ascertaining what the youth had observed, he left rather disappointed, telling the boy to keep on looking and maybe he would see something.

This put the boy on his mettle, and he began to work with his pencil, putting down little details that had escaped him before, but which now seemed very plain to him. He began to catch the secret of observation. Little by little he brought to light new objects of interest about the fish. But this did not suffice his teacher, who kept him at work on the same fish for three whole days. At the end of that time the student really knew something about the fish, and, better than all, had acquired the "knack" and habit of careful observation and perception in detail.

Years after, the student, then attained to eminence, is reported as saying: "That was the best zoological lesson I ever had—a lesson whose influence has extended to the details of every subsequent study; a legacy that the professor left to me, as he left to many others, of inestimable value, which we could not buy, and with which we cannot part."

Concentration of attention can be exercised in three fields or spheres of reality. It can be outward-directed, as in observing some natural object like a fish, in studying an issue, or in performing an action. It can also be inner-directed, when used to become aware of and to analyze subjective psychological states: one's thoughts, fantasies, or drives. It can also be upward-directed, when the center of consciousness, the "I," directs its inner gaze toward higher, superconscious processes and the Transpersonal Self. This last kind of concentration is needed for carrying on the inner activity of meditation and for maintaining a state of contemplation.

While concentration generally, and especially at first, requires a definite act of will, after some time it can persist on its own without any effort or tension of the will itself. This is the case when one is absorbed in the contemplation of the beauty of some natural object or scenery, or is in the state called by the mystics "passive contemplation" or "orison of quiet."

An important and practical use in carrying out willed acts of concentration combined with control consists in maintaining clearly and steadily the images and ideas of the actions one wills to perform in the field of consciousness. This implies the voluntary utilization of the motor potential inherent in images and ideas as expressed in the psychological law "Images or mental pictures and ideas tend to produce the physical conditions and the external acts that correspond to them."

Both the way this law works and how it can best be used are dealt with in the chapter on the Skillful Will. Concentration, like all other qualities and functions, can be developed by appropriate exercises and kept at an effective level by constant use. Many exercises for developing concentration could be mentioned, but I think that it is not necessary because all the exercises described in the chapter on the Strong Will require concentration and serve to train and develop this quality.

4. Determination—Decisiveness—Resoluteness—
   Promptness

This quality of the will is demonstrated chiefly in the

stage of Deliberation.* The lack of decisiveness and resoluteness is one of the weaknesses of democratic systems, where deliberation can become an endless process. We know how difficult it is to induce a large assembly to arrive, if not at unanimity, at least at a majority decision. There are well-known historical examples of this ineffectiveness of assemblies; one concerned the Roman Senate: it was said that *"Dum Romae consulitur, Seguntum expugnatur"* ("While the Roman Senators indulged in consultations, the enemy conquered the town of Seguntum"). Another and amusing example is that of the cardinals gathered for the election of a pope in Viterbo. They discussed and fought for months until finally the people became impatient and angry and uncovered the roof of the hall where the cardinals were assembled. After this, the decision was quickly made.

But one must be careful not to confuse promptness and rapidity with impulsiveness. Impulsiveness doesn't stop to deliberate at all; it jumps over, so to speak, the stage of deliberation, sometimes with fatal consequences. Therefore, it is important to have deliberation, but without too much lingering; not to decide is also a decision, and may turn out to be the worst one.

Determination, decisiveness, and resoluteness are also much needed at the stage of the Execution of the willed act. It has been said that one of the reasons for the success of Napoleon was his rapidity of decision. The Italian philosopher Niccolò Tommaseo says that resoluteness is an essential component of the strength of will. Resoluteness is closely related to another quality of the will which we are going to consider later: *initiative, courage, daring.*

* The stage of Deliberation in the act of will is discussed at length in Chapter 13.

5. Persistence—Endurance—Patience

For certain tasks of great length, steadfastness of purpose and persistence are needed even more than energy. In fact, they may aptly replace energy in persons who have little physical strength. In this case, one may effectively use the technique of "little and often." That is, of accomplishing one's work in small installments, with short and frequent rests taken at the onset of fatigue. In such a way, Charles Darwin completed his monumental *Origin of Species*, thus compensating for the fact that his physical energy was so low that he usually could not work much more than an hour a day.

Another kind of persistence is that exercised in spite of repeated failures. This is the secret of many successful inventors and scientists. It is said that Edison tried about two thousand substances before finding carbon wire for making his electric bulb. Let us think how much we owe him for this extraordinary persistence. He would have been well justified if he had given up the attempts at the thousandth or even the five hundredth trial.

This kind of persistence can be called *tenacity*. Other instances of tenacity are those of authors who offer their manuscripts to several publishers in spite of repeated refusals. An outstanding and amusing example is that of Jules Verne, the pioneer of science fiction. When he was twenty-five and had just completed his first novel, he went with the manuscript under his arm, knocking at the door of fourteen publishers, all of whom laughed in his face. Finally the fifteenth, Hetzel, took the manuscript in order to read it. After ten days, Hetzel not only pledged himself to publish the novel but offered Verne a contract for twenty years for a book each year. The fortune of Verne was made, and also that of Hetzel.

Persistence, tenacity, and repetition can be seen also in the natural world. There is a Latin saying that "the drop makes a hole in the stone not through its force, but by its constant falling." This is a principle well understood by advertisers and dictators. Like many qualities of the will, persistence can be put to bad or good uses. It is successfully and well used in one technique employed by psychosynthesis: repetition.

Another form of persistence is that of *endurance*. It is outstandingly demonstrated in the endurance of physical hardships, in sport in general, especially in mountain-climbing, and recently was admirably apparent in the astronauts. It is a saving quality when one finds oneself in protracted painful and unavoidable conditions. One outstanding example of endurance is that of Viktor Frankl's willed survival of Nazi concentration camps, vividly described in his book *From Death Camp to Existentialism*. Such heroic cases can help us overcome any tendency toward grumbling, self-pity, and giving up when faced with much much lesser physical hardships or adverse conditions. From the existential viewpoint, the attitude of endurance can be called "willingness to accept suffering." It has been found that the refusal to accept suffering can often create neurotic conditions, while generous acceptance of unavoidable suffering leads to insight, growth, and achievement.

Another form of persistence is *patience*. This quality is generally not associated with will because of a limited understanding of what the will entails, but patience is part of the fully developed will. Many authors have patiently written and rewritten parts of their work until they were satisfied that it was as good as they could make it. Hermann Keyserling, who was a prolific and easy writer, and generally revised very little or not at all, said that when he worked at what he himself rightly considered his most important work, *Méditations sud-américaines,* he rewrote some of the chapters six or seven times each. And Hemingway, who also generally wrote fluently without revising, rewrote one of his short stories several dozen times.

6. Initiative—Courage—Daring

This quality has two roots: one is the recognition that full and lasting security is fundamentally an illusion. There is no complete security in our life, physical, financial, or of other kinds. So the craving for security at any cost is self-defeating. It is a bourgeois attitude, against which, at present, there is a healthy reaction, particularly among the young.

The other incentive toward courage is the enhancement and stimulation given by danger, by risk. This often brings a feeling of intense aliveness and clarity and can create a true expansion of consciousness and even an ecstatic state. Such experiences have been described by some mountain-climbers, parachutists, deep-sea divers, and astronauts. Of course, risks should not be reckless and thoughtless; here also there is a danger of overdoing, and of taking needless chances that have no purpose except the emotional excitement they give. Courageous risk-taking is justified and appropriate when it has a well-thought-out purpose and value, but is not primarily an end in itself.

7. Organization—Integration—Synthesis

This quality of the will is, in a certain sense, the most important, the one which enables it to fulfill its unique and *specific* function. This function and the way it operates may be illuminated by an analogy with a healthy body. In the body there is a marvelous coordination of the activities of every cell, organ, and groups of organs, the function and purpose of which are to keep the body alive and active. The body shows an intelligent cooperation of each element, from the cells to the large functional systems such as the circulatory system, the digestive, and so on. There is a complex interaction and mutual balancing of the activity of the endocrine glands, regulated by the nervous system in order to create a condition of equilibrium and to maintain it in spite of all disturbing impacts from the external world. Thus the body is a unified organism, a functional unit of countless diverse parts—a perfect demonstration of *unity in diversity*.

What is the unifying principle that makes this possible? Its real nature escapes us; we can only call it *life;* but something can be said of its qualities and ways of operating. They have been variously called *coordination, interaction,* or *organic synthesis.* According to the mathematician Luigi Fantappiè, this principle is one of the manifestations of the general law of *syntropy,* or *negative* entropy, of which he has given a precise mathematical formulation verified by observations. Syntropy is beginning to be recognized as a fundamental principle of nature, one having far-reaching, universal implications. Buckminster Fuller states, "My continuing philosophy is predicated, first, on the assumption that in counterbalance to the expanding universe of entropically increasing random disorderliness there must be a universal pattern of omnicontracting, convergent, progressive orderliness, and that man is that anti-entropic reordering function. . . ."

Teilhard de Chardin gives ample evidence of this law, which is at the basis of all evolution—biological, psychological, and spiritual—and produces what he calls "complexification" and "convergence." He describes the various stages of this process of synthesis—which in humanity becomes conscious—toward and including a superindividual * and cosmic center which he calls *the omega point.*

If we consider this process "from within," we find that we can have a conscious existential experience of it. We can experience it as an *intelligent energy,* directed toward a definite aim, having a *purpose.* These are also the specific characteristics of the *will* as an expression of the synthesizing *self.* We need not discuss how the unifying, synergetic force operates at the biological levels. What matters is to realize that we can be aware of its higher manifestations in the conscious human being, and also at transpersonal levels. This quality of the will operates in various ways. First, as an inner synergy, coordinating the various psychological functions; it is the unifying force which tends toward, and enables one to achieve, personal psychosynthesis. It is also active at the transpersonal level and works toward the unification of the personal center of consciousness, the "I" or ego, with the Transpersonal Self, leading to the corresponding harmonious cooperation of the personal will with the Transpersonal Will (transpersonal or spiritual psychosynthesis).

The will demonstrates synergy also in the outer activities of the individual, in his acts of willing, both in coordinating and organizing those activities through Planning and Programing (the fifth stage of the will in action) and in Directing and Regulating the successive phases of their Execution (sixth stage).

* Here a semantic clarification is needed in order to avoid confusion and misunderstandings. While psychologists such as Jung use the term "individuality" to describe the higher aspects of the human being, to be attained through what they call a process of "individuation," Teilhard de Chardin, adopting the terminology generally used by Christian writers, uses the words "personality" and the process of "personalization" to describe the higher aim above and beyond the "individual."

The operation of the laws of cooperation, organization, and synthesis is evident not only in the intrapersonal realm but also in the large field of interpersonal relationships, from the couple to all social groups and finally the whole of humanity. Its expressions have been variously called empathy, identification, love, social will. It tends to transcend the opposition between the individual and society, the selfish-unselfish polarity. Maslow called the transcendence of this dichotomy "the creation of a superordinate unity."

Finally, there is the planetary and cosmic synergy which—by analogy—can be surmised to be the expression of the deliberate action of the will of corresponding transhuman principles or entities, as Teilhard de Chardin asserts. This, according to him, is the logical, necessary goal of the whole evolutionary process. I had arrived at the same conclusion before knowing Teilhard de Chardin's writings, and had expressed it in my paper "Psychoanalysis and Psychosynthesis," published in 1934 in *The Hibbert Journal*, and later included in my book *Psychosynthesis* under the title "Dynamic Psychology and Psychosynthesis":

> From a still wider and more comprehensive point of view, universal life itself appears to us as a struggle between multiplicity and unity—a labor and an aspiration towards union. We seem to sense that—whether we conceive it as a divine being or as cosmic energy—the Spirit working upon and within all creation is shaping it into order, harmony, and beauty, uniting all beings (some willing but the majority as yet blind and rebellious) with each other through links of love, achieving—slowly and silently, but powerfully and irresistibly —the *Supreme Synthesis.*

4

THE STRONG WILL

As we have seen, the strong will is in a sense the most basic as well as the most familiar aspect of the will. In the strength of the will lies its power, its impetus, its energy. In developing the strength of the will we make sure that a willed act will contain enough intensity, enough "fire," to carry out its purpose.

As with other functions, the strength of the will can be developed and increased through practice and exercise. However, may I emphasize again that while strength is an important aspect of the will it is *only one* of its aspects; therefore, at the same time that we try to increase the strength of the will, let us work as well at developing all the other aspects: the skillful will, the good will, and the Transpersonal Will.

Since the strong will is already familiar to most of us, I will begin, without further description, to discuss some of the practical methods and exercises which can be used for developing it. To ensure success in training the will generally, a proper preparation is needed for arousing the initial urge and impetus; this preparation should produce a lively, fervid, and intense desire to develop the will, leading to the firm decision to do all that is necessary for attaining that end. This in itself requires a certain amount of will; but, fortunately, all of us have at least *some* will, and although it may only exist in an embryonic state, still it is sufficient for a beginning to be made. This firm determination can result from the initial urge and impetus of a strong desire to develop the will.

EXERCISES FOR STRENGTHENING THE WILL

I. *Realizing the Value of the Will*

Settle yourself into a comfortable position with your muscles relaxed.

A. Picture to yourself as vividly as possible the loss of opportunity, the damage, the pain to yourself and others which has actually occurred, and which might again occur, as a result of the present lack of strength of your will. Examine these occasions, one by one, formulating them clearly; then *make a list of them in writing*. Allow the feelings which these recollections and forecasts arouse to affect you intensely. Then let them evoke in you a strong urge to change this condition.

B. Picture to yourself as vividly as possible all the *advantages* that an effective will can bring to you; all the benefits, opportunities, and satisfactions which will come from it to yourself and others. Examine them carefully, one by one. Formulate them with clarity and *write them down*. Allow the feelings aroused by these anticipations to have full sway: the *joy* of the great possibilities that open up before you; the *intense desire* to realize them; the *strong urge* to begin at once.

C. Picture yourself vividly as *being in possession* of a strong will; see yourself walking with a firm and determined step, acting in every situation with decision, focused intention, and persistence; see yourself successfully resisting any attempt at intimidation and enticement; visualize yourself as you will be when you have attained inner and outer mastery.*

II. Evoking Feelings Toward the Will

This exercise consists of using *reading material* particularly suited to the cultivation and reinforcement of the feelings and the determination aroused by the previous one. The material should be encouraging, positive, and dynamic in character, and apt to arouse self-reliance and to incite to action. Very suitable for this purpose are biographies of outstanding personalities who have possessed great will, and books and articles intended to awaken the inner energies. But in order to get full benefit from such a course of reading it must be performed in a special way. Read slowly, with undivided attention, marking the passages that impress you and copying those that are most striking or which seem specially adapted to your case. The following quotation from Emerson's "Self-Reliance" has been useful to many:

There is a time in every man's education when he arrives at the conviction that envy is ignorance; that imitation is suicide;

* This is the technique of the "Ideal Model." The exercise as a whole is based on the technique of visualization, because of its value and effectiveness in any creative process. See the discussion of the Ideal Model and Visualization in my *Psychosynthesis*, pp. 166–77, and 145–51.

that he must take himself for better, for worse, as his portion; that though the wide universe is full of good, no kernel of nourishing corn can come to him but through his toil bestowed on that plot of ground which is given him to till. The power which resides in him is new in nature, and none but he knows what that is which he can do, nor does he know until he has tried.

It is worth while to reread these passages several times, absorbing their full meaning.

These exercises create the inner condition, produce the inner fervor needed for making the decision to devote the time, energy, and means necessary for the development of the will.

A word of warning: do not talk about this matter with others, not even with the laudable intention of inducing them to follow your example. Talking tends to disperse the energies needed and accumulated for action. And if your purpose is made known to others, it may provoke skeptical or cynical remarks which may inject doubt and discouragement. *Work in silence.*

This preparation lays the ground for the following exercises, which are aimed at the direct strengthening of the will.

The Gymnastics of the Will

III. "Useless" Exercises

The foundation of the method is simple. Every organ of our body and every function can be developed by exercise. Muscles become stronger by a series of contractions. In order to strengthen a specific muscle or group of muscles, as in the case of a weakened limb, there are exercises arranged in such a way as to put into motion only that weak part of the body. In a similar manner, in order to strengthen the will, it is best to exercise it independently of every other psychological function. This can be accomplished by performing deliberate acts which have no other purpose than the *training* of the will. The application of such seemingly "useless" exercises has been strongly advocated by William James in these terms:

> Keep alive in yourself the faculty of making efforts by means of little useless exercises every day, that is to say, be systematically heroic every day in little unnecessary things; do something every other day for the sole and simple reason that it is difficult and you would prefer not to do it, so that when the cruel hour of danger strikes, you will not be unnerved or unprepared. A self-discipline of this kind is similar to the insurance that one pays on one's house and on one's possessions. To pay the premium is not pleasant and possibly may never serve us, but should it happen that our house were burnt, the payment will save us from ruin. Similarly, the man who has accustomed himself steadily, for day after day, to concentrate his attention, to will his energy, for instance, not to spend money on unnecessary things, will be well rewarded by his effort. When disasters occur, he will stand firm as a rock even though faced on all sides by ruin, while his companions in distress will be swept aside as the chaff from the sieve.

Later, Boyd Barrett based a method of will training on exercises of this sort. It consists in carrying out a number of simple and easy little tasks, with precision, regularity, and persistence. These exercises can be easily performed by anyone, no special conditions being required. It is enough to be alone and undisturbed for five or ten minutes every day. Each task or exercise has to be carried out for several days, usually a week, and then replaced by another in order to avoid monotony and the formation of a habit leading to automatic performance. Here is an exercise of this kind, quoted from Boyd Barrett's book *Strength of Will and How to Develop It*:

Resolution—"Each day, for the next seven days, I will stand on a chair here in my room, for ten consecutive minutes, and I will try to do so contentedly." At the end of this ten minutes' task write down the sensations and the mental states you have experienced during that time. Do the same on each of the seven days. . . .

The following are excerpts from reports contained in the book:

1st day: Exercise a little strange, unnatural. Had to smile or cross my arms and stand akimbo in order to feel contented. It was arduous to me to hold myself in an attitude of voluntary satisfaction doing nothing. Naturally I was distracted by various thoughts, for instance, "What will this experience lead to?", etc.

2nd day: The time of the exercise passed easily and agreeably. I had a sense of satisfaction, of pride, of virility. I feel "toned up" mentally and physically by the mere fact of exercising my will, and by holding in my resolution.

3rd day: Have had a sense of power in performing this exercise imposed by myself on myself. Joy and energy are experienced in willing. This exercise "tones me up" morally, and awakens in me a sense of nobility, and of virility. I maintain an attitude, not of submission and resignation, but of willing actively what I am doing, and it is this that gives me satisfaction.

Boyd Barrett proposes several other exercises of the same kind:

1. Repeat quietly and aloud: "I *will* do *this*," keeping time with rhythmic movements of a stick or ruler for five minutes.
2. Walk to and fro in a room, touching in turn, say, a clock on the mantelpiece and a particular pane of glass for five minutes.
3. Listen to the ticking of a clock or watch, making some definite movements at every fifth tick.
4. Get up and down from a chair thirty times.

5. Replace in a box, very slowly and deliberately, one hundred matches or bits of paper (an exercise particularly adapted to combat impulsiveness).

Similar techniques can be invented ad libitum. The important thing is not the doing of this or that exercise, but *the manner* in which it is performed. It should be done willingly, with interest, with precision, with style. Try always to improve the quality of the work, the clearness of introspection, the fidelity of the written account, and above all to develop the awareness and the energy of the will. It is good to compete with oneself; in other words, to assume a "sporting attitude" in the best sense of the word.

IV. Physical Exercises in the Strengthening of the Will

These constitute a very effective technique when used with the specific intention and purpose of *developing* the will. As the French writer Gillet has expressed it, "Gymnastics are the elementary school of the will . . . and serve as a model for that of the mind." In reality, every physical movement is an act of will, a command given to the body, and the deliberate repetition of such acts—with attention, effort, and endurance—exercise and invigorate the will. Organic sensations are thus aroused: all produce a sense of inner strength, of decision, of mastery that raises the tone of the will and develops its energy. However, to extract from such exercises the fullest benefit, it is necessary that they be performed with the exclusive aim, or at least with the principal objective, of training the will.

Such exercises must be performed with measured precision and attention. They should not be too forceful or too fatiguing; but every single movement or group of movements must be executed with liveliness and decision. Exercises or sports best fitted for this purpose are not the ones of a violent and exciting nature, but rather those that call for endurance, calmness, dexterity, and courage, permitting interruption and variety of movement. Many outdoor sports—such as golf, tennis, skating, hiking, and climbing—are particularly suitable for the training of the will; but where they are not possible, physical exercises can always be carried out in the privacy of one's room. There are many books or manuals dealing with the techniques of body movement.

V. Exercises of the Will in Daily Life

Daily life, with its many tasks and occupations, presents countless opportunities for developing the will. Most of our activities can be helpful in this way, because through our purpose, our inner attitude, and the way in which we accomplish them, they can become definite exercises of the will. For instance, the mere fact of rising in the morning at a definite time can be of value, if for that purpose we rise ten or fifteen minutes earlier than usual. Also, getting dressed in the morning can be such an opportunity, if we accomplish the various necessary movements with attention and precision, swiftly but not hurriedly: "calm rapidity" is a useful watchword. To make haste slowly is not easy, but it is possible; and it leads to greater effectiveness, enjoyment, and creativeness without tension and without exhaustion. It is not easy because it requires a dual attitude and awareness: that of "the one who acts" and simultaneously that of the one who looks on as the observer.

During the rest of the day one can do numerous exercises for the development of the will which at the same time enable one to unfold other useful qualities. For instance, remaining serene during one's daily work, no matter how tedious the task may be; or controlling acts of impatience when confronted with minor difficulties and annoyances, such as driving in heavy traffic, or being kept waiting, or noticing the mistakes or faults of a subordinate, or being unjustly treated by a superior.

Again, when we return home, we have the opportunity for similar simple valuable exercises: controlling the impulse to give vent to our bad temper caused by various vexations, preoccupations, or business worries; dealing serenely with whatever comes our way; and trying to adjust disharmonies in the home. At the dinner table, an exercise no less useful for health as for the will is to control the desire or impulse to eat quickly while thinking of business, etc., training ourselves instead to chew well and to enjoy our meal with a relaxed and calm mind. In the evening we have other occasions for training, such as when we want to resist the allurements of people or things that would make us waste time and energy.

Whether away at business or in the home, we can resolutely cease working when tired, controlling the hurry to get a job finished. We can give ourselves wise rest and recreation; a short rest taken in time, at the outset of fatigue, is of greater benefit than a long rest necessitated by exhaustion.

During these rest periods, a few muscular exercises or relaxation for a few minutes with closed eyes will suffice. For mental fatigue, physical exercises are generally the most beneficial, and each individual can find out by practice what suits him best. One of the advantages of such short interruptions is that one does not lose interest in, or the impetus for, the work in hand, and at the same time one overcomes fatigue and nervous tension. An ordered *rhythm* in our activities generates harmony in our being, and harmony is a universal law of life.

One of the chief difficulties in developing a will which is weak is the lack of will with which to work! It is helpful in this situation to engage temporarily the cooperation of some of the personal drives, such as pride or ambition, which may provide a stronger incentive than the pure will. One of the best incentives is the instinct to play—the sporting attitude of a contest with oneself creates a drive which, being interesting and amusing, does not arouse the resistance or rebellion that would result from a forceful imposition of the will.

A word of warning: it is not necessary, or even desirable, to do all of these exercises at once. It is, rather, advisable to begin with only a few, spread over the day, beginning with the easier ones. When success has been achieved with these, one can gradually increase their number, varying and alternating them, performing them cheerfully and with interest, scoring successes and failures, setting oneself records and trying to beat them in a competitive, sporting spirit. Thus the danger is avoided of making life too rigid and mechanical, rendering instead interesting and colorful what otherwise would be tiresome duties. All with whom we are associated can become our cooperators (without their knowing it!). For instance, a domineering superior or an exacting partner becomes, as it were, the mental parallel bars on which our will—the will to right human relations—can develop its force and proficiency. Delay in being served with a meal gives us the opportunity to exercise patience and serenity, as well as the chance to read a good book while waiting. Talkative friends or time-wasters give us the chance to control speech; they teach us the art of courteous but firm refusal to engage in unnecessary conversations. To be able to say "no" is a difficult but very useful discipline. So the Buddhist saying goes: "An enemy is as useful as a Buddha."

5

THE SKILLFUL WILL:
PSYCHOLOGICAL LAWS

Modern psychology has shown that if the will puts itself in direct opposition to the other psychological forces, such as the imagination, emotions, or drives, it will often be overpowered. Yet the limited Victorian conception of the will as force alone prompts us to use our will in just such a direct and often clumsy, or even brutal, way. Or, as a reaction, we may swing to the opposite extreme of not using the will at all.

In other words, as we have said, there are two general mistakes caused by extreme attitudes held toward the will and its relation to the other psychological functions. One is the traditional attempt to force these functions into operation by sheer power and direct imposition. The other mistake, which is prevalent today, is to abdicate the will: urges, drives, and desires are allowed to "happen," without any regulation or consistent direction. In such a situation, the function that is strongest at the moment will capture one's attention and express itself, and in so doing will inhibit or repress all the other less powerful functions. This produces inner conflict and stress, reduced effectiveness through dispersal of energies, and potentially harmful reactions within oneself and between oneself and others.

We can avoid both these mistakes when we realize and remember that the will is capable of achieving its purpose provided it is not only strong but also skillful.

The essential function of the skillful will, which we need to cultivate, is the ability to develop that strategy which is most effective and which entails the greatest economy of effort, rather than the strategy that is most direct and obvious. For example, if we want to get a car going and we get behind it and push with all our strength, we use a will which is only strong. But if we sit in the driver's seat, turn on the ignition, and drive the car, we use a skillful will. In the first case we have a considerable probability of failing, and even if successful, we will have needlessly expended a considerable amount of energy. We will have made a very unpleasant effort which may leave us temporarily exhausted, and we will certainly do our best to avoid repeating such an experience in the future. In the second case, we are guaranteed success with a bare minimum of effort—provided we have previously acquired an understanding of the car and sufficient skill in handling it.

The most effective and satisfactory role of the will is not as a source of *direct* power or force, but as that function which, being at our command, can stimulate, regulate, and direct all the other functions and forces of our being so that they may lead us to our predetermined goal. But, just as with the car, for this we need to have some understanding of the psychological world *in* which, and *on* which, the will has to operate. With this understanding, we can choose the most practical, effective, and effort-saving means and strategies to proceed along our way. We need to know the basic *elements* of this psychological world, the *forces* active in it, and the *laws* that regulate the willed act. This knowledge leads to the skillful direction of the intended activity of the will, and enables us to make countless practical applications of those psychological laws, under the direction of the will.

In the remainder of this chapter we will deal with these psychological elements, forces, and laws. In the next chapter we will present a number of specific techniques and their rationale, for the use of the skillful will. These techniques, which can be seen as examples illustrating the general principles we have discussed, have been chosen because of their effectiveness in a broad range of everyday life situations. Therefore, besides representing typical utilizations of the basic concepts and methods of the skillful will, they will offer the reader practical means to develop and exercise his own skillful will, and to appreciate its value out of personal experience. As one gains increased proficiency and familiarity, one can then proceed to modify these techniques as desired for his individual needs, and to develop new ones.

Psychological Elements

The general psychological structure of the human being, the relationship between the personal I and the Transpersonal Self, and the relationship between the area of awareness and the surrounding unconscious have been briefly indicated in Chapter 2 (see diagram, page 14).* But it is also necessary to be aware of the various psychological functions and their relationship to one another.

* It seems unnecessary to repeat here the full discussion of these points to be found in *Psychosynthesis*, pp. 16–22.

Many classifications of them have been made, but I consider the following to be the most inclusive: 1. Sensation; 2. Emotion-Feeling; 3. Impulse-Desire; 4. Imagination; 5. Thought; 6. Intuition; 7. Will. They are represented once again in the following diagram, in which the specific and central position of the will is indicated:

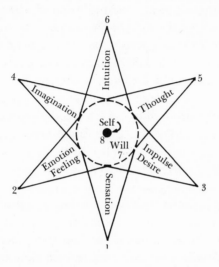

The relationships among these functions are complex, but there are two kinds of interactions: first, those that take place spontaneously, one might say mechanically; second, those that can be influenced, governed, and directed by the will.

Psychological Forces

This leads to a consideration of the difference between what can be called the "plastic" unconscious and the "structured," or "conditioned," unconscious. In classical psychoanalysis the emphasis is on the latter: detecting repressions, complexes, conflicts, and attempting to eliminate them are the chief aims. But there is a large portion of the unconscious which is *not* thus conditioned; it is plastic, and its susceptibility to being influenced makes it like an inexhaustible store of unexposed photographic film. The conditioned unconscious, on the other hand, can be compared to an accumulation of already exposed film. In this respect we are like motion-picture cameras functioning uninterruptedly, so that at every moment a new section of the sensitive film is receiving impressions of the images which happen to appear before the lens.

But the new impressions thus received do not remain in a static condition. They *act* in us; they are living forces that stimulate and evoke other forces, in accordance with the psychological laws which will be enumerated in the next section. This may be looked at from a different angle, by employing another analogy. Just as our body is continually absorbing vital elements from the outer world, from the air, from light, water, and from various foods, and these elements exercise various influences upon it according to their nature—be they beneficial or harmful, wholesome or unwholesome—so in the same way our unconscious is continually absorbing elements from the psychological environment. It breathes, as it were, and unceasingly assimilates psychological substances whose nature determines whether their effects upon us are beneficial or harmful. According to the Hindus:

> *Sarvam annam,* everything is food. We feed not only on vegetarian or non-vegetarian food, but on all sound and visual vibrations, on all kinds of impressions: architectural proportions, union of forms and colors, harmonies and rhythms of

music and all the ideas with which we come in contact. All this, absorbed mechanically and without real attention throughout the day, has made up our being and continues to do so.

But we can also learn to use these influences skillfully, to build in ourselves what we choose to have. For their dynamics are regulated by laws as definite as those governing physical energies.

The various psychological functions can interpenetrate and interact, but the *will* is in a position to *direct* their interpenetration and interaction. The centrality of the will allows it supremacy through its regulating power, but this power is in turn governed by psychological laws. Ignoring these laws means to waste, or to risk misusing, the inherent power which the will, because of its centrality, has. So knowledge of these laws, and the use of techniques based on them, is of fundamental importance. We will enumerate here those which have a practical bearing on the use of the will. I believe that knowing these laws and some of their practical applications, which we will discuss in the next chapter, provides a firm basis for anyone who would train his will to act skillfully. The reader may want to study the laws once and then return to them later to solidify his understanding.

Law I—Images or mental pictures and ideas tend to produce the physical conditions and the external acts that correspond to them.

This law has been formulated also in the following way: *"Every image has in itself a motor element."* Every idea is an act at an initial stage. William James was one of the first to call attention to "ideo-motor" action, in which a central idea releases, triggers, and gives life to the waiting muscular system.

The existence of this law, or process, has been abundantly proved by the effects of hypnotic influence, and in the waking state, of suggestion and autosuggestion. To the objection that one is often not aware that images and ideas transform themselves into actions, the reply can be made that this is because, ordinarily, numerous mental pictures crowd in on us at the same time or in rapid succession, conflicting with and hindering each other. This law is at the base of all psychosomatic influences, both pathological and therapeutic, and it is one of the facts which account for mass suggestion, so cleverly and successfully exploited by advertisers and other "persuaders," including political leaders.

The centrally located will can mobilize the energies of imagination and of thought, and utilize these energies within the individual to carry out its plan. So the will can be used purposefully and consciously by the individual to choose, evoke, and concentrate on the images and ideas that will help to produce the actions he desires. For example, images or ideas of courage and high purpose, used skillfully, tend to evoke courage and produce courageous acts.

Law II—Attitudes, movements, and actions tend to evoke corresponding images and ideas; these, in turn (according to the next law) evoke or intensify corresponding emotions and feelings.

This is clearly proved by the following experiment: if we shut the fist of a sensitive hypnotized subject, he will gradually shut the other fist, raise his arm, close his lips tightly, and frown, until his entire aspect will suggest a growing inner state of anger. We know that to "play a role" in life tends to arouse the corresponding ideas and feelings; thus, speaking with a harsh voice and behaving as if one were angry tends to awaken real anger. One often sees this in children who begin to fight for fun, but gradually become so involved that they end by fighting in earnest.

This law provides the basis of the method used by some people to penetrate into and understand the psychological conditions of others. They artificially imitate the body posture and facial expression of someone they are observing, and in so doing arouse in themselves the corresponding psychological conditions.

Thus, the will can move the body, and by this means evoke corresponding images and ideas, which in turn will intensify the emotions and feelings it wants to strengthen. In other words, through conscious and purposeful movements, one can evoke and strengthen positive and desired inner states. The use of appropriate dance movements and the Eastern technique of "mudrā" are typical applications of this law. A skillful use of the body under Law II can further strengthen the motor power (Law I) of images and ideas.

For example, the individual who is working to develop and express courage by utilizing his imagination and his thoughts according to Law I can also use his body purposefully by assuming the corresponding physical attitude. Thus his body will intensify and reinforce his imagination and thoughts, according to Law II, and this will in turn evoke and intensify the experience of courage itself, creating a reinforcing flow of energies, a positive feedback loop, which will lead him to the sustained performance of courageous action. This law and its application will be expanded further when we discuss the technique of "acting as if" in the next chapter.

Law III—Ideas and images tend to awaken emotions and feelings that correspond to them.

This relates closely to Law I. Ideas and images tend to produce *acts* in accordance with the first law, and *emotions* in accordance with this law. Whether acts or emotions are first awakened by a specific idea or image depends on the nature of the idea or image itself, and on the individual psychological type. Again, with a skillful application of this law the centrally located will can mobilize the energy of the emotions and feelings through the use of appropriate ideas and images. The technique of "evocative words," described at length in the next chapter, is a systematic application of this law, but examples abound from clinical practice, history, and many other spheres of life.

A young man was addicted to morphine but earnestly wanted to get rid of this slavery. He was advised to write twenty times every day a verse from a certain psalm. He did it faithfully until, after having written it about seven thousand times, he felt and remained free from the craving. Seven thousand may seem a very large number, but it corresponds to less than a year's time. Another famous story concerns the daughter of an English admiral who read a pamphlet by Gandhi and became so enthused with his ideas that she left for India, much to the disgust of her father. There she became Gandhi's active co-worker and for years was his secretary. One may say that the ideas of Gandhi aroused deep feelings, and these, in turn, according to Law IX and Law X which I discuss below, led to action.

Law IV—Emotions and impressions tend to awaken and intensify ideas and images that correspond to or are associated with them.

The emotions evoked through ideas and images (Law III) can in turn awaken and intensify associated ideas. Here, too, we have a feedback process which can operate for good or for ill. It often works negatively; for example, a fear of becoming ill breeds a series of images of illness which are harmful, both because they are depressing and still more because the mental pictures thus evoked tend to produce the corresponding physical conditions, i.e., psychosomatic troubles (through the action of Law I). So we are caught in a vicious circle where an emotion creates an image which in turn affects the physical condition, which produces more emotions. We can break this circle in one of several places in accord with the laws we are considering. If we wish to begin by dealing with the emotions, the technique that is most useful is that of self-identification described in Appendix One (page 211).

Law V—Needs, urges, drives, and desires tend to arouse corresponding images, ideas, and emotions. Images and ideas, in turn (according to Law I) prompt the corresponding actions.

One of the most widely occurring examples of this law is what is termed in psychoanalysis "rationalization." When a strong desire or urge exists, it influences the mind to find reasons, or rather pseudo-reasons, for its fulfillment. This process is also at the root of the general tendency to wishful thinking. Once we are aware of this law, we can be on the alert for the possibility of the mental and emotional illusions produced by rationalization. We can learn to become more aware of our drives, urges, and desires and what they want us to do. Instead of being swept along with them or fooled into believing they are justified by valid reasons, we can examine these pseudo-reasons and decide for ourselves, from the central vantage point of our wills, whether or not we want to follow them.

For example, if as I am about to give a lecture to a

large audience I suddenly think of a very "good" reason to leave the stage and go home, I can remember this law and become aware of the compelling inner urge working on me. I might then choose to use one of the other psychological laws, imagining myself delivering a good lecture in a confident manner, thus calming my emotional agitation and also mobilizing myself to perform the willed action. If the will is used skillfully there is no need to repress negative feelings or to override them harshly. Such procedures are inefficient and demand too high a price.

Law VI—Attention, interest, affirmations, and repetitions reinforce the ideas, images, and psychological formations on which they are centered.

Attention renders images and ideas *clearer* and *more exact*, and enables new elements and details to be found. It may be compared to a lens through which we observe an object. The image is made larger, clearer, and sharper. That which is at the center of attention is well defined, whereas what is at its circumference remains dim. (The latter can be termed "marginal consciousness"; it belongs to a semiconscious sphere, an intermediate zone, between the conscious and the unconscious.)

Interest increases the *prominence* of ideas and images. It makes them occupy a *larger space* in the field of our consciousness and remain in it for a *longer span of time*. It enhances and reinforces attention. Conversely, attention tends to increase interest (this is also a feedback process).

Affirming images and ideas gives them stronger force and effectiveness.

Repetition acts like the blows of a hammer on a nail and brings about the penetration and fixation of an idea or image, until it becomes dominant and even obsessive. This is a technique much in use by advertisers; the huge sums they spend with profit in putting the same advertisement frequently before the eyes of the public are convincing proof of the effectiveness of repetition.

There can be also an opposite utilization of this law. We can deliberately *withdraw* interest and attention from an unwanted image, idea, or psychological formation, and thus gradually de-energize it and reduce its activity. It will then cease to be a disturbing factor or a harmful influence. Several applications of this principle, in particular the *technique of substitution,* will be found in the next chapter in the section on "Psychological Breathing and Feeding."

Law VII—Repetition of actions intensifies the urge to further reiteration and renders their execution easier and better, until they come to be performed unconsciously.

In this way *habits* are formed. They can be compared to streets and roads: it is so much easier and more convenient to walk along a street than to force one's way through the undergrowth of uncultivated land. As repeated habitual actions are taken over by the unconscious, the conscious is freed for other and higher activities. This is an established fact in the case of the biological functions. And Gustave Le Bon, in his book *La Psychologie de l'éducation,* goes so far as to state that "education is the art of making the conscious pass into the unconscious." While this is true of learning and skills, it is certainly not the aim of all education. One might say just the contrary in regard to its higher aspects. The etymology of "education" (*e-ducere*) expresses its true purpose and function: to "draw out" the latent possibilities from the unconscious, to activate the energies dormant in it, particularly in its higher sphere, the superconscious.

Habits tend to limit us and make us follow only beaten tracks. But, as William James has aptly said, "Will and intellect can form habits of thought and will. We are responsible for forming our habits and even when acting according to habits we are acting freely."

Law VIII—All the various functions, and their manifold combinations in complexes and subpersonalities, adopt means of achieving their aims without our awareness, and independently of, and even against, our conscious will.

This law has been called by Baudoin the "Law of Subconscious Finalism," and he has fully described its workings and explained the ways of utilizing it in therapy and education in *Suggestion and Autosuggestion.* It is a law of fundamental importance. We should realize that we are seldom conscious of the psychological and psychophysiological mechanisms which produce physical changes and outer actions. Here we have the real mystery of the relationship and interaction between psychological and physical facts, which, despite all attempts, has not yet been satisfactorily solved or explained.

The simplest and clearest evidence is provided by any muscular movement. A man, let us say, wills to move, or has the idea of moving, an arm. He does it easily, though he may be completely ignorant of the complex and admirably coordinated mechanism which converts the idea into the act. The idea, or mental picture, of the arm movement produces a stimulation of the motor cells in the cortex of the opposite hemisphere of the brain. From these motor cells an impulse, which seems to be of an electrical nature, starts and flows through the fibers until it finally reaches the muscles involved in the movement. That stimulation produces the contraction of the muscle fibers which activates the movement. A man with strong muscles can perform the movement as easily as, and more effectively than, a learned anatomist or physiologist with a weak body.

The same holds true not only for all psychophysical reactions but for all the activities going on in the psyche itself. Complex and more extended processes also follow the same pattern; the mental picture of the aim to be attained starts an activity in the unconscious directed toward the accomplishment of the aim. But we remain ignorant of their operation. Creativity, whether artistic, scientific, or technical, is a case in point. It often requires a period of elaboration, or incubation, during which it is advisable to let the unconscious work without further interference from the conscious will. Paradoxically, paying conscious attention to, or being emotionally preoccupied with, creative processes disturbs them. What happens may be compared with an executive giving a worker a certain job to do. Once the worker has understood what has to be done, he should be allowed to do it without further interference or prodding.

This shows the nature of spontaneity. From a certain point of view, the activity in the unconscious can be said to go on spontaneously, that is, spontaneously from *our* point of view, and without our conscious cooperation. Many creative artists and investigators have had practical experience of the working of this law. Providing the initial impetus, they allow the further elaboration to occur naturally and spontaneously. But this is quite a different matter from the "cult of spontaneity" as expressed in uncontrolled giving way to any emotion, impulse, or whim.

Law IX—Urges, drives, desires, and emotions tend and demand to be expressed.

Drives and desires constitute the active, dynamic aspect of our psychological life. They are the springs behind every human action. But their origin, nature, value, and effects differ widely; these must therefore be recognized and then examined with the same objectivity with which one studies a natural object. The procedure necessitates disidentification from them, at least temporarily, and this in turn means acquiring awareness of the self, the conscious "I," as distinct from these psychological elements and forces; and from that central point observing their flow. An act of will is called for here, and the will, as we have seen, is the most immediate and direct function of the "I."

Observation has to be followed by *valuation*. Science, particularly psychological science, cannot avoid valuation. A. H. Maslow has presented the reasons for this ably and convincingly in his books *The Psychology of Science* and *Motivation and Personality*.

The practical problem, the issue that confronts us all the time, is this: how to give adequate and constructive, or at least harmless, expression to each of these urges, drives, emotions, etc. To give some expression to them is necessary. If we fail to do so, if fear, condemnation, or other motives induce us to deny or repress them, they produce psychological and nervous stress, and, by affecting the body, are apt to create psychosomatic disorders. This fact has been strongly emphasized by psychoanalysis and on it is based the present claim to eliminate all inhibitions and checks to the free course of the energies lumped together under the general term *libido*.

Yet this uncontrolled expression is often not desirable

in view of the harmful consequences it can have for oneself and other people, and in many cases it is not even possible. But there are a number of methods by means of which the impelling drives may be given harmless or constructive expression. Their value, multiplicity, and diversity demand that they be thoroughly known, carefully selected, and appropriately applied, in accordance with the specific existential situations that continually confront us in life. The law which follows deals with these methods.

Law X—The psychological energies can find expression: 1. directly (discharge—catharsis) 2. indirectly, through symbolic action 3. through a process of transmutation.

1. At first sight the *direct modes* of expression do not appear to call for much comment. They are simply the means whereby the natural and healthy gratification of the fundamental needs and tendencies is obtained. But in reality things are not that simple. Conflicts often develop between these needs and tendencies, conflicts placing priorities and limits on their gratification, or even negating its feasibility. Moreover, these tendencies cannot all be indulged at the same time; their expression needs to be *regulated* on the basis of criteria of possibility and suitability. And this, in turn, necessitates deliberation, choices and decisions, in fact *acts of will.*

Certain restrictions inevitably impose themselves because of individual physical and psychological circumstances, obstacles created by our relations with other people, and social and environmental conditions in general. But these problems of control and regulation are not insoluble. When, and to the extent that, *direct* expression must be delayed, modified, or even entirely disallowed, ways and means of *indirect* expression are at hand which can offer adequate satisfaction and may often be preferable.

2. A *symbolic* acting out is frequently just as satisfying and liberating as direct expression. For example, if anger provokes us to attack somebody we believe has treated us badly, its direct expression would involve us in a physical or verbal assault. But the same hostility can be discharged by trouncing some object that symbolizes our opponent.

Another way of discharging hostility is to write a vituperative letter giving full vent to one's bitterness and resentment—and then not to send it! The mere action of expressing anger and indignation on paper is often sufficient to discharge the energy, or psychological voltage, it carries.

3. *Transformation and sublimation.* These processes have a special importance in that their recognition and utilization offer the best and more lasting solution to many basic human problems. This warrants their thorough investigation and wide application. The breadth of the subject does not permit of its being adequately dealt with in the present context, but some of the essential points are presented here.

The transformation of energies is a natural process going on at all times, both "horizontally," *within* each level—physical, biological, and psychological—and "vertically," *between* all levels, where it can be seen as *sublimation* or *degradation,* according to whether energy is carried to a higher or lower level. These transformations often occur spontaneously, but they can be induced by deliberate acts of the will. At the physical level, heat may be converted into motion (the steam engine) or electricity (the thermo-electric generator). Electricity in its turn can be converted into heat (the electric stove) and motion (the motor). The knowledge and utilization of these and many other transformations constitutes the basis of technology.

Chemical combinations of substances produce other substances having different properties from those of their components and in some cases bring about a simultaneous release of heat and energy. In the physical sciences there is a process, called sublimation, through which a chemical substance passes from the solid state directly to the gaseous state, and after cooling, to final crystallization. It is interesting to note that sublimation of chemical elements is particularly valuable as a means of purification.

At the biological level countless transformations are constantly occurring or can be induced, all regulated in the wonderful ways that make life possible. At the psychological level, too, transformations are happening all the time. Many of the phenomena governed by above-mentioned laws are due to the interaction and transformation of psychological energies.

Most important—though their mechanism is still a mystery to us—are the transformations and interactions that take place vertically, that is, between the energies of the various levels. Of immediate interest are the biological and physical changes produced by the action of mental and psychological energies. Their study and utilization constitute the large field of psychosomatic medicine.

There are then all the external actions determined by psychological factors. An idea combined with a desire or a feeling arouses an impulse to set in motion the corresponding physical activities. For instance, the desire for wealth in conjunction with a plan for acquiring it may prompt one to make a journey, embark upon some enterprise, or construct a building. Love for a woman allied with an assessment of the conditions for marrying her has been known to transform itself into the urge to pursue certain studies or the determination to obtain a particular job.

All the basic instincts and drives undergo such transformations, which are particularly evident in the case of:

Self-assertion and *aggressiveness*.

Sexuality and *love*.

The transformation of combative and aggressive drives has a central importance because it constitutes one of the most effective, perhaps the most effective, means of eliminating interpersonal conflicts and preventing war. As to sexuality and love, there is certainly no need to emphasize the fact that the ways to deal with these two powerful drives is an existential problem confronting every human being. This subject has been treated in *Psychosynthesis* (Chapter VIII), and in my pamphlet *The Transformation and Sublimation of Sexual Energies*.

The ways and means of psychological transformation and sublimation can be summed up as:

A. Elevation; B. Purification; C. Interiorization; D. Extension; E. Outer expression.

A. By means of *elevation* the merely physical sex drive can be transformed into emotional love; possessive love into oblative love; craving for sensuous pleasure into aspiration to experience aesthetic, intellectual, and spiritual joys.

B. *Purification* is concerned principally with the nature of motives and intentions.

C. *Interiorization* can transmute vanity and pride into a sense of inner dignity; personal self-assertion into spiritual affirmation; aggressive drives into a tool for dealing with inner "enemies." This use has been aptly stated by Frances Wickes: ". . . one of our great tasks of our present day—[is] to introvert war."

D. *Extension* brings about the transformation of egotistic love in successive, wider circles to love of family, of fellow workers, of one's country, and of humanity. Paternal and maternal love which may have been denied expression through lack of children can be bestowed upon those of others, or upon all people who may need love and help.

E. *Outer expression* corresponds to the "crystallization" of sublimated chemical substances. Thus compassion is expressed in humanitarian actions; aggressive tendencies can be utilized in the struggle against social evils. It is important to realize, however, that there are pseudo-sublimations, which should be recognized and guarded against. They are a substitute, a counterfeit of the real thing; they can be a disguise covering over impulses and activities not really sublimated. In sublimation it is sincere *intention* that counts. Pseudo-sublimation is present where there is hypocrisy, whether evident or not.

The process of artistic creativity deserves special mention. It is considered a form of sublimation; it often is, but not always. In his creative activity the writer, painter, or composer often gives expression to his drives, urges, and desires as well as to his aspirations. For him it is then a means of catharsis. On the nature and level of this expression depends the quality of the transformation of the energies involved.

6

PRACTICAL APPLICATIONS
OF THE SKILLFUL WILL

The number of these applications is practically endless. A wide range of specific psychological techniques based on the laws given in the previous chapter have been developed and tested in the field, and are available for implementation,* while new ones are being continually developed. It might be said that they include the whole field of applied psychosynthesis. While an exposition of them is outside the scope of this book, I will describe a few in some detail as typical examples, and for their outstanding usefulness in a variety of common situations.

I. Realizing the Value of the Will

This exercise, discussed on pages 36–37 as a preliminary to the "Gymnastics of the Will," is itself based on the skillful use of the will. In performing it we apply the existing strength of our will, no matter how small, to act on our *imagination*, and use its power to realize the great value of having an effective will. This *realization*, in turn,

* They are described in Part II of my book *Psychosynthesis.*

arouses *urges, desires,* and *emotions,* all aligned with our initial intention, that is, with the original direction of our will. This procedure of vividly imagining the limitations and drawbacks of an existing condition we want to change, and the advantages of changing it, is very valuable to generate momentum before initiating any kind of inner or outer activity. It is a psychological analogue to power steering, or to the servo brakes of an automobile, or to the many other devices that, by means of mechanical advantage, allow man to augment his physical strength by practically any desired amount.

II. Technique of Substitution

Most of us have had the experience, at some time or other, of some thought, tune, verse, or sentence which captures our attention and is able to hold it for a long period of time, occasionally for hours, despite our attempts to get rid of it. In extreme forms, this condition can even become pathological. And if, in trying not to think about something, we concentrate directly on "not thinking about it," it will tend, perversely, to become more central and vivid in our awareness. Yet if we choose any *other* subject or image and direct our attention to *it,* we find that the unwanted thought will gradually become more peripheral and tenuous, and eventually fade away all together.

This is a simple application of the *technique of substitution.* It is based on Law VI, page 56, according to which *attention* centered on an object gives it *energy,* making it more important to our awareness. Continued attention tends to increase *interest* and interest in turn reinforces the attention, thus creating a positive feedback loop. When the unwanted thought or image draws our awareness, it becomes like a magnet that captures our attention and continues to draw increasing energy from it. So if we pit the strength of our will directly against it, we are likely to fail. But if we use a more skillful, less direct and "aggressive" approach, by deliberately building another such center of attraction, we can easily use it to liberate our captive attention.

It might be argued that all we are doing is to displace our attention from one image to another. This is certainly the case, but the point is that the second image is the one of our choice, and we can choose that it be of greater usefulness than the first one. So this technique has practical application in dealing with all kinds of annoying, disturbing, and negative recurrent thoughts or images, as well as with undesired or harmful influences.

Of course, a word of caution should be given here. As with any technique, substitution may be misused, applied without a clear perception of an individual's existential situation, or without a good sense of appropriate timing. Certain recurrent images and thoughts which are negative and disturbing are clues that an emotional block may exist, and in these cases, if substitution is used before the difficulty has been sufficiently explored, understood, and dealt with, it may tend to suppress the material which is trying to emerge into consciousness. On the other hand, even when the problem has been brought to the surface, worked on, and largely resolved, these images often linger on at a relatively low level of energy, like an old tune, or an old habit. In this case substitution is especially appropriate and effective, for it can help to clear away the debris and make free and clear space in consciousness. Much of the inner clutter in which we try so hard to live and work can be dealt with by this technique of substitution.

It can also be useful in regulating and counterbalancing excessively one-sided tendencies within ourselves. This is a more subtle application of the skillful will. The technique of substitution is utilized also in the more general method of *psychological breathing and feeding,* described next.

III. Psychological Breathing and Feeding

More than a specific technique, this constitutes a general approach to our everyday life, which can be implemented most effectively through the application of the skillful will.

In many ways our psychological needs resemble our physiological needs. We know that our physical health depends on a number of basic factors, such as a balanced diet, the regulated ingestion and assimilation of food, and the breathing of clean, pure air. We have gained considerable skill in the basic principles of personal hygiene, and in recognizing and avoiding—or protecting ourselves from—those environmental situations that can produce infection, communicate contagious diseases, or otherwise cause physical harm. Many of the recent, most promising activities in the field of ecology can be seen as an extension of this attitude—and of a personal sense of responsibility as well—to include all of humanity and our whole planet.

In the psychological field, on the other hand, our awareness is lagging far behind. A general recognition of the powerful psychological influence of our environment, to which we are all subject, is still lacking, even though the major problems of today, such as war, the increasingly harmful competitive attitude, and the widely prevalent conditions of fear and depression, either belong to, or have their causes in, the psychological domain.

Yet at least a beginning in this direction is being made,

and a small but rapidly growing minority of people are developing what might be called a psycho-ecological conscience. An interesting indication of this emerging awareness is the use of the word "vibration" by many young people. The terms "good vibrations" and "bad vibrations" are increasingly used to describe what is considered as a favorable or unfavorable psychological environment or condition.

It seems very timely, therefore, to indicate some of the more common *harmful factors* which pollute our psychological environment, and to suggest skillful-will methods by which we can most effectively deal with them. The principal negative factors are *aggressiveness and violence; fear; depression and despondency; greed and all forms of selfish desire*. They are true "psychological poisons" which permeate the psychic atmosphere, and careful examination will find them at the root of a very large number of difficulties, both within the individual and within society.

In order to deal with them effectively, we need to remember that these psychological poisons exist not only in external surroundings but also, to a greater or lesser degree, *in all of us*. We need therefore to eliminate them also *within* ourselves, or reduce them to a minimum. This is a specific task of individual psychosynthesis, and it calls for different techniques from those suitable for gaining protection from *external* poisons.

To be most effective, the two operations should be performed side by side. This is because on one hand, it is practically impossible to reach such a degree of freedom from internal poisons as to be completely immune to the influence of those coming from the outside world. On the other hand, external poisons tend to feed and intensify the corresponding ones in us. Thus a vicious circle comes into being: the poisons within us open the door to the influence of external ones, while the latter intensify the former. A most effective way to break the vicious circle is to *withdraw* attention deliberately from these psychic poisons. This will liberate the energy of the attention and allow it to be focused elsewhere, in a direction where it will do the most good. The act of this withdrawal of attention is a definite act of the skillful will and in turn contributes to strengthening the will itself.

1. Aggression and Violence

The widespread aggression and violence now un-leashed throughout humanity are too evident to need pointing out. The first remedial step is to stop inten-sifying them by unnecessarily focusing attention and interest on them. Yet newspapers, magazines, television programs, and films vie with each other in presenting vivid and dramatic accounts of events and scenes of aggression and violence. All this emphasis can only serve to intensify aggression through the agency of what has been called the "feeding power of attention." It would thus be a measure of elementary psychological hygiene, of protection of our mental health, to avoid or at least greatly limit exposure to sensational accounts and illus-trations of this kind.

This does not mean closing our eyes to aggression and violence, or ignoring their existence. It is one thing to deal with objective information about such conditions for a useful purpose, and quite another to submit ourselves, needlessly and indiscriminately, to a flood of sensational descriptions and pictures.

2. Fear

This, too, is a widely diffused poison. Besides personal fears and anxieties, waves of collective fear and panic invade the psychic atmosphere. One of these waves is aroused by the peril of global warfare and the consequent destruction of human life on a vast scale. Also widespread is apprehensiveness about economic crises and unemployment, epidemics, criminality, civil violence, and so on. Here again the first and pressing thing to do is to avoid exacerbating and feeding these fears with unfounded prophecies of catastrophe and to turn our attention purposefully and firmly to areas that are positive and constructive.

It is only as we free ourselves from the overwhelming sweep of collective panic about all of these vital issues that we are truly able to do something about them. So, paradoxically, a person who is sincerely and deeply concerned with bettering economic conditions, ending war, or the like, will be most effective if he does not open himself completely, even in the name of compassion, to all these influences, but rather is able to maintain a centered and calm focus on specific issues so he can clearly see what needs to be done.

3. Depression and Despondency

These are reactions to much that is negative, "dark," unjust, and unsatisfying within collective human life. While these conditions have always existed, the present period is witnessing their significant increase, to which the mass-communications media are giving an exaggerated and one-sided emphasis. Some respond to these evils with aggression and the urge to destroy the old system by violent action. The reaction of many others, on the other hand, is one of depression, even despair, produced by a feeling of frustration and uselessness.

4. Greed

A fourth kind of psychological poison can be entered under the general heading of greed. Greed is an expression of *selfish desire* which, according to Buddha's teaching, is at the root of all suffering and unhappiness. Such suffering occurs not only because many desires are unrealistic, and thus can never be gratified, but even more because of the very nature of greed, which is such that no satisfaction lasts for long; it always demands something more.

There are many kinds of desire. One, the drive toward *excessive* and unbridled *self-assertion,* is one of the major causes of aggression and violence. Another is *excessive sensuality,* in the broadest sense an inordinate craving for physical pleasures of all kinds. Of this, gluttony—to employ an old-fashioned but expressive term—is a typical expression. The intake of food and drink greatly in excess of bodily needs or unsuited to individual constitutions is too frequently responsible for ill-health and premature loss of life. The analogy between food intake and sexual activity has been pointed out by Maslow in the following terms:

> An excellent parallel may be made between this and the attitude of these (self-actualizing) people toward food. Food is simultaneously enjoyed and yet regarded as relatively unimportant in the total scheme of life by self-actualizing people. When they do enjoy it, they can enjoy it wholeheartedly and without the slightest tainting with bad attitudes toward animality and the like. And yet ordinarily feeding oneself takes a relatively unimportant place in the total picture. These people do not need sensuality; they simply enjoy it when it occurs.

Let us be clear that neither eating nor sexual activity are "poisons" in themselves. They are natural functions and are inherently necessary for the preservation of the individual and humanity's very life. The pleasure derived from their healthy gratification is good, and it can be enjoyed wholeheartedly, without any sense of guilt.

When I speak of poison, I mean the *attachment* that leads to *excesses,* and above all the *exploitation* promoted for commercial purposes which leads to such excesses. We are continually bombarded from all directions by intensive suggestion to make us purchase food and drink, and by an emphasis on sexuality, which is a paramount ingredient of modern books, illustrations, films, television, and pseudo-art. Thus an exaggerated and *artificial* stimulation of the sex drive is created, one which is completely different from the healthy, spontaneous natural instinct. This is a distinction that must be clearly recognized.

Another factor connected with sexuality is its current dissociation from the rest of the human personality, particularly from its affective aspect. Sexual dissociation manifests the generally committed error of failing to recognize and take into practical account the vital connections linking the various aspects and levels of the human being. In this way physical, emotional, and mental activities become alienated from one another and come to function separately, causing conflict and inner discord.

It is well to be quite clear on the point that no drive, emotion, or desire needs to be repressed or should be condemned on its own account; it is the skillful *regulation* of its use and manifestations that is needed. Any medicine can become a poison if used unsuitably and in excessive doses, whereas some strong poisons given in minimal doses are curative in appropriate cases. It is precisely the regulatory function of the skillful will that finds here one of its most useful fields of action.

A sound psychological hygiene demands the avoidance of these poisons, as much as possible, through the use of the skillful will, and then collective action to eliminate them. A campaign against the sources of *psychological* smog and pollution, parallel to the present ecological campaign, urgently needs to be started. It might be objected that, while one lives in the world, one cannot withdraw completely out of range of these influences; this is true, but it can be done within certain limits. In many cases one can deny them attention and interest. Moreover, exposure to them may be counteracted by "disinfectant" measures, during and after. Doctors and nurses working in departments of infectious diseases are not afraid of infection, but take precautionary measures (gloves, masks, use of disinfectants, etc.). Similarly, we can have recourse to disinfectants and precautions against psychological poisons.

What methods are to be used by the skillful will to achieve psychological hygiene? The fundamental one consists, as I have said, in *withholding attention and interest.* Most people can do this to a considerable extent, once they understand the advantage of it. So it can be of great help to foresee in clear terms the harmful consequences of absorbing such poisons. An even more powerful approach is the already mentioned method of *substitution:* the cultivation of other, better interests, the systematic focusing of the attention on constructive things. This tends to give immunity to the negative, harmful, or poisonous influences. A most effective method, explained by Patanjali in his *Yoga Sutras*, is *neutralization,* which entails the active cultivation of qualities that are the antithesis of the harmful ones: harmlessness and nonviolence in the face of violence; courage in place of fear; joy in healthy pleasures instead of depression and despondency; moderation as a substitute for greed. As for overemphasis on sexuality, the most effective antidote is true love. It is thus not a question of not loving, or of loving less, but of loving *better*.

IV. The Technique of Evocative Words

That certain words, such as *serenity, courage, joy, compassion,* have their effects on our moods and ideas does not require demonstration. All words are symbols that not only indicate or point out objects or psychological facts but also possess the power of stimulating and arousing activity associated with them. They "evoke" and make operative the meanings and *idées-forces* that they signify. This process follows principally three of the laws referred to in the last chapter. (Laws I, VI, and VIII, pages 51, 56, and 58). According to these laws, every idea or image tends to produce the state of mind, the physical state, and the acts that correspond to it; attention and repetition reinforce the effectiveness of the idea or image; the effects of the idea or image, i.e., the activation of that which it signifies, are produced without our being aware of them. By using the technique of evocative words we can apply these laws under the direction of the skillful will.

The first step in using evocative words is to choose the one that expresses the quality we want to evoke and develop. We can then put a card with that word printed on it in a place where it will be easily noticed and where it will readily catch the eye: at the bedside, on a desk, on a table, or on a wall. Even if we do not consciously pay attention to it, the visual image produces an impression on our psyche, or more precisely on our plastic, receptive unconscious, and gradually works on it. A stronger cumulative effect can be obtained by placing several cards with the same word in different places and rooms. This might be called a "beneficent obsession"!

Bringing conscious attention to bear on the word

provides an even more effective method. This can be done in various ways:

1. Assume a state of relaxation and then observe the word attentively for a period of one or two minutes. If ideas and images associated with the word emerge from the unconscious, let them come and record them.

2. Reflect on the meaning of the word, and then record the results.

3. Try to "feel" the psychological quality that the word embodies, letting it permeate yourself, if possible even to the point of identification with it.

4. While observing the word, say it aloud, or murmur it.

5. Write the word many times.

These methods combine visual, auditory, and motor images and thereby increase the effectiveness of the exercise.

The choice of which word to use can be made in one of two ways: either by deliberately choosing a word that corresponds to the quality that one desires to arouse and develop, or by choosing a word at random from a group of such words and adopting it as the "password" for the day, or for the period decided upon. The rhythm to be adopted may be either continuous use of the same word for a certain time—a week, a month, or more—followed by its repetition after an interval, or rapid rotation, i.e., the use of a different word in the series every day.

The preference to be given to one or the other of these different methods depends not only on an individual's objective, but also on his psychological type. So it is advisable to experiment with a number of them, and then adopt the one that is most attuned to one's own constitution, or that seems most rewarding.

The following list includes some of the most often used evocative words. Others can be added to suit individual needs.

admiration • appreciation • attention • beauty • bliss • brotherhood • calm • compassion • comprehension • cooperation • courage • creativity • daring • decisiveness • detachment • determination • discernment • discipline • endurance • energy • enthusiasm • eternity • faith • freedom • friendship • generosity • goodness • good will • gratitude • harmony • humor • inclusiveness • infinity • initiative • integration • joy • liberation • light • love • order • patience • peace • persistence • positiveness • power • promptness • quiet • reality • renewal • resoluteness • serenity • service • silence • simplicity • synthesis • tenacity • truth • understanding • universality • vitality • wholeness • will • wisdom • wonder**

Such a use of words represents the simplest and most elementary application of a general method whereby psychological energies are employed to modify and direct states of mind and human behavior. Some of the techniques which can be used for this purpose are displays of posters of large size; suggestive phrases and slogans; "persuasive" and striking pictures; musical themes or excerpts that are associated with related words or phrases; and rhythmic movements, gestures, and dances that symbolically express a message.

This is the method of suggestion, or, as it is at present more euphemistically called, of "persuasion," so widely and effectively used for commercial ends, and by means of which we are continually, and often unknowingly, led to act in ways that bring gain to others, although they

---

* Some evocative phrases can be found at the end of the chapter on affirmation, page 177. Cards of some twenty commonly used words, printed in different colors and accompanied by a pamphlet with detailed instructions for their use, are available, as packages, from the Psychosynthesis Research Foundation, 40 East Forty-ninth Street, New York, New York.

may cause harm to ourselves. It is an effective example of the application of the skillful will, which is not necessarily accompanied by the good will. But such techniques can well be just as effectively and systematically employed for higher and more constructive purposes. They can be used by any individual for his own growth, by a psychotherapist or teacher to help those he is guiding, and can eventually lead to the organization and execution of widespread and intensive eupsychian publicity campaigns directed toward individual and collective improvement and the uplifting of humanity.

A word of caution is needed here. Sometimes the words are apt to arouse negative reactions. Some people will resent the simple appearance of a card with a pleasant word like JOY, CONFIDENCE, SERENITY, or COURAGE. They feel as if the words are preferring charges against them, as if the words are making them painfully aware of their lack of these qualities, and this irritates them. Sometimes *both* a positive and negative reaction is aroused (ambivalence). Consciously there may be just a negative reaction, while the unconscious is favorably impressed; or, vice versa, the word can be appreciated by the conscious ego but arouse resistance or antagonism from unconscious factors. It is well to become aware of such ambivalent reactions and to deal skillfully with them in appropriate ways.

V. The "Acting As If" Technique

This technique consists in *acting as if* one actually possessed the desired inner state.* It is based on the fact that, while the will can exercise only a limited *direct* control over emotions and feelings, and often no control

* I will further discuss the appropriateness of using this technique on pages 142–44.

at all, it can act much more directly and fully on physical attitudes and external actions. If, for example, we are sad or depressed, it is difficult, if not impossible, to become cheerful or serene through a *direct* act of will. On the other hand, it is within our power to smooth our forehead, lift our head, smile, and speak words of harmony, optimism, confidence, and joy. That is to say, we are able to *behave* "as if" we were cheerful and confident. Doing so gives first of all a feeling of freedom, and confirms that we are not the slaves of our ever-changing emotions, of our physiological and psychological conditions, which react to so many external causes— environmental circumstances, other people's influence, or the difficulties or uncertainties in a given situation.

Thus we can, to a large extent, act, behave, and really *be in practice as we would be* if we possessed the qualities and enjoyed the positive mental states which we would like to have. But this is not all. More important, the use of this technique *will actually change our emotional state.* Little by little, and sometimes rapidly, the emotional state will follow, adapt itself to, and match the attitude and external behavior. Tommaso Campanella used to imitate the facial expressions and gestures of people when he wanted to know what they were feeling. This, he had found, was a way of arousing corresponding feelings in himself. The operative law here is the second (see page 52): *"Attitudes, movements, and actions tend to evoke corresponding images and ideas; these, in turn (according to the next law) evoke or intensify corresponding emotions and feelings."*

The psychophysiological mechanism of this phenomenon can be explained in this way: every external act requires that it be first imagined or visualized, even if unconsciously. But then during its performance the self-observation that accompanies it creates an image that, in its turn, produces a reinforcing effect, a positive feedback process. It could be said that the "as if" technique makes use of the same dynamic power of images as in suggestion, only in a reverse direction. In suggestion the images arouse the feelings and emotions and then the corresponding actions. Acting "as if," instead, one proceeds from the external act, which has been determined by the direct action of the will, to the image of the act itself, and from the image to the corresponding emotional states.

One often employs this technique spontaneously. It is common knowledge that whistling helps to keep up one's courage in a lonely place at night. Singing, or getting others to sing, is a well-known spur to action. Machiavelli and Buffon both used to don gala dress when about to write, having found that their styles reflected the attitude and mental state created by their costumes.

There are examples of the use of this technique being implemented by determined acts of will, with successful and sometimes surprising results. The French general Turenne provides a historical one. His custom of marching resolutely in front of his troops going into battle earned him a reputation for great courage. (They made war like that in those days.) Someone once complimented him on his courage and Turenne replied, "Of course I *conduct* myself like a brave man, but all the time I'm feeling afraid. Naturally, I don't give in to the fear, but say to my body, 'Tremble, old carcass, but walk!' And my body walks."

Turenne's behavior demonstrated that the higher form of courage does not consist in having no feeling of fear, but in acting "as if" one had none. A still more striking example of the effectiveness of the technique is given by Goethe, and deserves to be related in his own words:

I found myself in a state of health which furthered me sufficiently in all that I would and should undertake; only there was a certain irritability left behind, which did not always let me be in equilibrium. A loud sound was disagreeable to me, diseased objects awakened in me loathing and horror. But I was particularly troubled by a giddiness which came over me every time that I looked down from a height. All these infirmities I tried to remedy, and indeed, as I wished to lose no time, in a somewhat violent way. In the evening, when they beat the tattoo, I went near the multitude of drums, the powerful rolling and beating of which might have made one's heart burst in one's bosom. All alone I ascended the highest pinnacle of the Minster spire, and sat in what is called the neck, under the roof or crown, for a quarter of an hour, before I would venture to step out again into the open air, where, standing upon a platform scarce an ell square, without any particular holding, one sees the boundless prospect before, while the nearest objects and ornaments conceal the church, and everything upon and above which one stands. This is exactly as if one saw oneself carried up into the air in a balloon. Such troublesome and painful sensations I repeated until the impression became quite indifferent to me, and I have since then derived great advantage from this training, in mountain travels and geological studies, and on great buildings, where I have vied with the carpenters in running over the bare beams and to cornices of the edifice, and even in Rome, where one must run similar risks to obtain a nearer view of important works of art. Anatomy, also, was of double value to me, as it taught me to tolerate the most repulsive sights, while I satisfied my thirst for knowledge. And thus I attended also, the clinical course of the elder Doctor Ehrmann, as well as the lectures of his son on obstetrics, with the double view of becoming acquainted with all conditions, and of freeing myself from all apprehension as to repulsive things. And I have actually succeeded so far, that nothing of this kind could ever put me out of my self-possession. But I sought to steel myself not only against these impressions of the senses, but also against the infections of the imagination. The awful and shuddering impressions of the darkness in church yards, solitary places, churches and chapels by night, and whatever may be connected with them, I contrived to render likewise indifferent; and in this, also, I went so far that day and night, and every locality, were quite the same to me; so that even when, in later times, a desire came over me once more to feel in such scenes the pleasing shudder of youth, I could scarcely force this, in any degree, by the strongest and most fearful images which I called up.

This drastic method of Goethe's, however, is not within the capacity of everyone, for it presupposes the possession, or the previous development, of a strong and determined will. But the "as if" technique can be applied gradually and facilitated by the help of other techniques. This is a course strongly advocated and frequently applied in psychosynthesis. When a particular technique by itself fails to obtain a desired result, various ones in combination can succeed. In fact, the art of harnessing a selected "team" of techniques in the same undertaking may be said to be a specific task of the skillful, *wise* will.

When it is necessary or desired to overcome strong adverse tendencies or emotions, fear for instance, it is frequently helpful to precede the "acting as if" technique with that of the "ideal model." This entails visualizing ourselves as we would want to become, "seeing" ourselves in imagination acting in the manner in which we would like to act in actual practice. This method of self-training is similar to an actor's rehearsals, alone or with others, of the part he is to play later in public.

But when the performance of some action in reality is fraught with acute—or largely repressed—fear, it can often happen that this imaginative evocation has the result of magnifying such fear to the point of inducing a severe anxiety crisis. In such cases the preliminary use of another technique, that of "imaginative training," or "desensitization," will help to change the situation.*

Another technique, which can be used independently of, or in succession to, that of imaginative training, is *external* training. If one *gradually* accustoms oneself to doing something which at first arouses aversion, the unwillingness diminishes little by little, and finally disappears. This fact has an important and extensive application in the educational field. Parents should carefully avoid, if at all possible, forcing a child to do something which frightens it. They can instead teach it *by degrees* to get rid of the inhibiting aversion: for example, going into the sea to bathe, or, in the case of a very small child, walking, and so on. It is important to get a small child *gradually* accustomed to and familiar with what arouses fear, after which he can be persuaded to perform any appropriate action without the danger of repression. This is the proper approach also for adults who have some intense undesirable emotion, when there are means and time for applying it. But in cases of necessity in which sudden and unforeseen situations crop up and there is not time for this, one can "command" the body to "act as if" it did not feel the emotion. Let us call it "the Turenne method."

* It is described in *Psychosynthesis*, page 226.

7

THE GOOD WILL

In the preceding consideration of the development of the will, the individual has been regarded as an isolated unit, with his will as an instrument of personal achievement. But in reality the isolated man does not exist: he is in constant interaction with his family, his working associates, and society in general. His relationships are many and diverse.

However strong and able he may be, an individual who fails to take these relationships into consideration inevitably arouses reactions and conflicts that often defeat his aims. This seems obvious, yet modern life presents the spectacle of a general clash of wills on the part of those who compete for dominance in all fields. Class is in conflict with class, party with party, and nation with nation, while within the family unit there is frequent strife between husband and wife, between parents and children, and between relatives. Incalculable is the enormous wastage of physical and psychological energies, of time, money, and volitional energy, and incalculable is the sum of human suffering bred from these struggles. Truly, our civilization has adopted ways of life that not only are most improvident, but also run counter to the real good of each and all.

This is a matter of grave concern to humanitarians, and to all those who are "practical" in the deepest, widest sense. Thus many attempts are being made to replace competition with cooperation, conflict with arbitration and agreement, based on an understanding of right relations between groups, classes, and nations. All this is basically *a question of willing*. The success of these attempts depends on the gradual harmonization of the wills of all concerned. Such harmonization is difficult indeed, but it is possible; the differing individual aims *can* be made to fit into the circle of a wider human solidarity.

This more inclusive approach introduces a new aspect in the training of the will. We have seen how the individual will has the power to strengthen itself and skillfully direct the activity of the other psychological functions. Now the individual will faces another and higher task, that of *disciplining itself* and *choosing* such aims as are consistent with the welfare of others and the common good of humanity.

There are two methods of accomplishing this task:

> *The elimination of obstacles.*
> *The active development and expression of a good will.*

1. *Selfishness* constitutes the fundamental obstacle. Selfishness springs from the desire to possess and to dominate, which is an expression of the basic urges of self-preservation and self-assertion. Inevitably it comes into collision with obstructions that block its satisfaction; aggressiveness and violence are thereby aroused, and the will used to destroy whatever is interfering with the

attainment of the desired objects. Selfishness is inherent in man and has always existed; but in our present day it assumes more accentuated and dangerous forms because modern life provides stronger stimuli, fewer restraints, and more powerful instruments of destruction. The control of selfishness is therefore not only an ethical exigency; it is a necessity for the very safety of mankind.

A skillful use of the will can greatly assist this curbing of selfishness. Techniques abound; a number are described in Chapter VIII of my *Psychosynthesis* and can be applied to the curbing and to the transformation of aggressive drives. The problem with such a fundamental difficulty as the elimination of selfishness is not the lack of techniques, a number of which are available or can be developed by the thoughtful person. The problem, rather, is mobilizing the *will to good* so as to devote the required energy to this necessary aim.

2. *Self-centeredness.* While less obvious and crude than selfishness, it is also a great hindrance because of its tendency to refer everything to the personal self, to consider everything from the angle of one's own personality, to concentrate solely on one's own ideas and emotional reactions. It can be well hidden, since it can coexist with wholehearted attachment to others and with acts of sacrifice. The self-centered individual may not be and often is not at all *selfish*. He may be altruistic and sincerely want to do good. But he wants to do it *in his own way*. Therefore he is likely to be overbearing and fanatical. He attempts to convert everybody to *his* convictions, to impose *his* methods, and sees salvation only in the remedies *he* offers. Such an attitude is a fundamental error of perspective, a real "Ptolemaic" rather than "Copernican" outlook. Thus, with the best of intentions, he can do actual harm, like the kindly

monkey in the story, who, seeing a fish in the water, rushes to rescue it from drowning by carrying it up into the branches of a tree.

3. *Lack of understanding of others.* We are prone to misunderstand those who are of a different race, nationality, or social class; who belong to a different religion, political party, etc. But we often lack understanding no less in our attitude toward those nearest to us, toward those we love. Unfortunately personal love does not in itself, as many are apt to believe, create mutual understanding. We can often observe the sad spectacle of people who love each other dearly, but do not understand or appreciate one another's vital needs and thus cause each other great suffering.

The elimination of self-centeredness and lack of understanding—they are generally associated—calls for a complex and skillful approach. It requires primarily the *will-to-understand.* This, in turn, requires the *intention* to understand and also the *relinquishing* of the self-centeredness that prevents understanding of others. The *means* of arriving at such understanding are being furnished increasingly, though not yet adequately, by *humanistic psychology.* They include:

I. A knowledge of the general constitution of the human being. (This has been outlined in Chapter 2.)

II. A knowledge of *differential psychology* or the investigation of the psychological differences existing between individuals and between groups of individuals. A discussion of this subject can be found in Appendix Five (page 248).

III. *Empathy.* Regardless of one's intellectual understanding, genuine existential understanding is not possible without *empathy,* i.e., the projection of one's consciousness into that of another being. Its development and use demand an attitude of impersonality and self-forgetful-ness; it can be achieved by actively arousing, or letting oneself be pervaded by, an absorbing human interest in the person one *wills to understand.* It means approaching him or her with sympathy, with respect, even with wonder, as a "Thou" and thus establishing a deeper inner relationship.

This approach can deepen until it becomes first a living contact, and then a momentary or temporary identification. One can imagine oneself as having be-come—as being—that person. One can try to realize his thoughts, his feelings; picture oneself in various condi-tions and situations and evoke his mental and emotional reactions to them. Such empathy is made possible by the fact of the essential unity of human nature existing beneath, and in spite of, all individual and group diversities. In each of us there are, potentially, *all* the elements and qualities of the human being, the germs of all virtues and of all vices. In each of us there are the potential criminal and the potential saint or hero. It is a question of different development, valuation, choice, control, and expression.

Training in empathy not only helps one acquire a true understanding of others, but also bestows a wider human-ness. It gives an insight into the wonder and mystery of human nature, in which so many and such contrasting elements are found side by side; the core of goodness and the possibilities for change existing in the criminal, as well as the foibles, imperfections, and primitive drives to be found in every great man. We become aware of the conflicts going on within both these extreme human types and in all intermediate ones, and of the consequent suffering involved; and we recognize them to be similar to our own. Thus we are induced to drop the ordinary attitude of passing judgment on others. Instead a sense of wide compassion, fellowship, and solidarity pervades us.

From what has been said it is evident that the fullest possible understanding of others is an invaluable element in the exercise of the good will. With understanding comes the abandonment of the inclination to criticize, to judge, to condemn. With understanding is born the recognition that an individual "is as he is," and in a certain sense has the right to be what he is. For he is the product of an enormous number of collective and individual elements rooted in the past and the present, and of all kinds of conditioning over which he did not have control.

On the other hand, the individual is not fixed and immutable but is in a continual state of *becoming*. Everyone can direct and regulate his own "becoming" process to a certain extent; thus comes into play the *responsibility* he bears for the beneficent or harmful influence he has on other people. We are constantly influencing others, whether we are conscious of doing so or not, whether we desire to do so or not. And the more we are aware of this, the more we can see to it that our influence is beneficent and constructive. It all hinges on our *intention*. *"Intentionality,"* as Rollo May has emphasized, is a characteristic of the will. The good will is a *will* to do good; it is a will that chooses and wants the good.

It may be said to be an expression of love, and this raises the great problem of the relationship between love and will.

8

LOVE AND WILL

The Union of Love and Will

The danger of untempered will is that it lacks heart. We see, and used to see especially in Victorian times, the operation of a cold, stern, and even cruel will. On the other hand, love without will can make an individual weak, sentimental, overemotional, and ineffectual.

One of the principal causes of today's disorders is the lack of love on the part of those who have will and the lack of will in those who are good and loving. This points unmistakably to the urgent need for the integration, the unification, of love with will.

To treat the subject of love as fully as we have discussed the will would require another book. But a brief consideration of some of the most important meanings of the word is necessary if we are to understand the relationship between love and will.

Types of Love

The first love is love for oneself. Mention of this may occasion some surprise, as love directed toward oneself is generally considered to be synonymous with egotism or narcissism. This kind of self-love does of course exist, but it is not the only kind; here, as always, the great complexity and multiplicity of the human being must be taken into account. In the case of self-love, all depends on *what* we love in ourselves and *how* we love it. It is truly egotism if we love the egocentric and separative aspects in us, the craving of pleasure, possessions, and domination. But if we love what is higher and best in ourselves, what we *are* essentially, if we love our potentialities for growth, development, creative ability, and communion with others, then this love, devoid of egotism, urges us to live a life of higher quality. This love is then not only not an obstacle to loving others in the same way but, rather, a powerful means for doing so. As with all the types of love, self-love can be helped to regulate and direct itself by the will.

Love for other human beings is qualified by its *object.* *Maternal love** may be considered the first and fundamental human relationship. In its initial form, it has an *oblative* quality, manifesting the mother's willing devotion to the protection and care of her infant, a devotion in which the self-denial entailed is accepted joyously. However, the growth of the child is accompanied by the development of a healthy independence, which puts the purely maternal aspect of her love to a severe test. Her very devotion and sacrifice in the early days of the relationship now can turn into attachment and possessiveness. The son or daughter realizes this, even if unconsciously, and resents it. The more possessive and exacting the love of the mother, the more vigorous the

---

* The terms "maternal" and "paternal" are used here to indicate specific types of love. In most cases, both types will come from each parent, although in different proportions.

rebellion of the child. Conversely, the more oblative the love, the more durable and deep is the loving relationship. Again, the wise use of will can make all the difference.

Paternal love presents a parallel process, although with certain differences. Here, too, the father's basic love for his children has an oblative quality. But this initial eagerness to provide them with material and other help often gives place later to an urge to assert his authority and demand their obedience. Or else he may identify himself with a child to the extent of trying to mold him in his own image, an image which frequently is not particularly commendable! In other cases he may bring heavy pressure to bear upon his child to achieve what he himself has failed to accomplish, an unfair and usually unrealizable demand. The result in most instances is rebellion; when instead the child submits, he does so unwillingly, and his feeling of frustration can not only hinder his development but may damage or even kill the previous loving relationship.

Love between man and woman is another area in which much semantic confusion prevails. It is the cause of frequent, I would say incessant, misunderstanding and subsequent conflict. Some writers call love for a person of the opposite sex "erotic love," but the different meanings attributed to the word erotic render it ambiguous. In common parlance, as well as in much literature on the subject, eroticism is understood in a purely sexual sense, sometimes being employed virtually as a synonym for pornography. On the other hand, some philosophers and psychologists, harking back to the Eros myth and the meanings given to it by the Greeks, regard Eros as the attraction of one sex for the other, generated by a desire to unite and merge with the other person at all levels, particularly the emotional one.

In reality, love between men and women comprises a mixture of physical, emotional, mental, and spiritual attractions in proportions that differ substantially for every relationship and also change in the process of time. This explains the great difficulty two human beings experience in understanding one another, and in harmoniously uniting and integrating. Hence, the suffering and conflicts that ensue.

The most familiar and general aspects of this love are *passionate* love, *sentimental* love, and *idealistic* love. No less important, though traditionally given scant consideration in the choice of a partner, is the love founded on *intellectual* understanding and that born of *spiritual* communion.

Let us now turn to the class of love relationships other than those between people of opposite sex. Here we have *fraternal, altruistic,* and *humanitarian* love. While they can be aroused and intensified by a feeling of compassion for human pain, they derive fundamentally from a sense of essential identity with one's brothers in humanity. In some cases, such as "Franciscan love," it embraces all living creatures. A full treatment of these love relationships is contained in P. A. Sorokin's book *The Ways and Power of Love*, and in Martin Luther King's *The Strength to Love*.

There is also an *impersonal love,* a love for ideas or for ideals. In this, too, various components and aspects are present. Fascination with an ideal, or the beauty of an idea, often gives birth to a dedication and self-sacrifice of a high order. But it can also lead to fanaticism and the *idée-fixe*: a man may become obsessed by an idea or an ideal to the point of being blind to all else, incapable of understanding and cruel to those who do not share it or who oppose it.

Then there is a love so distorted that it might be called a caricature of love. It is the *idolatrous* love that takes the form of blind, fanatical admiration of the idols of the day, the stars of stage and screen, champions of sport, dictators and other leaders.

Finally, there is *love of God,* or whatever designation may be preferred to represent Universal Being or Being-ness: The Supreme Value, Cosmic Mind, Supreme Reality, both transcendent and immanent. A sense of awe, wonder, admiration, and worship, accompanied by the urge to unite with that Reality, is innate in man. Present in every age and every country, it has given birth to the many varieties of religious and spiritual traditions and forms of worship, according to prevailing cultural and psychological conditions. It reaches its flowering in the mystics who attain the lived experience of union through love.

Relationships of Love and Will

All these kinds of love have *specific* relationships with the will and its different aspects. The working out of these various relationships in the particular circumstances that each individual finds himself in is, obviously, one of the basic tasks of each of us. Much remains to be discovered in general and also in each individual case. Here I will make some observations only about the general nature of the most important relationships between love and will.

Love and will are generally present in individuals in inverse proportion. That is to say, those in whom love is predominant tend to possess less will and are little inclined to use what they have, while those endowed with a strong will often lack love or even exhibit its contrary. But this personal imbalance between love and will can be further accentuated by the essential differences in the *quality, nature,* and *direction* of the two aspects themselves. Love, being attractive, magnetic, and outgoing, tends to link and unite. Will, on the other hand, being "dynamic," tends by itself to be affirmative, separative, and domineering; it tends to establish a relationship of dependence. And clearly, these differences can lead to a real opposition.

Love is normally considered to be something spontaneous and independent of will, something indeed that "happens" in a manner that may run counter to our will. However true this may be at the beginning of an affective relationship, to cultivate human love that is satisfying, enduring, and creative is truly an art.

Human love is not simply a matter of feeling, an affective condition or disposition. To love *well* calls for all that is demanded by the practice of any art, indeed of any human activity, namely, an adequate measure of discipline, patience, and persistence. All these we have seen to be qualities of the will. If, as is commonly recognized, they are indispensable in mastering an art, be it playing an instrument, for example, or singing, or painting, or performing any other creative activity, whoever aspires to perfect himself in his chosen field will naturally be willing to devote to the required practice all the time and energy demanded. As yet, the necessity for the same degree of application in the sphere of love is largely ignored, or, if not denied, recognized only with reluctance.

The widespread incidence of misunderstanding and conflicts between those who enter into affective relationships provides ample evidence that "falling in love" and merely sexual and emotional attraction are insufficient for achieving successful loving. The establishment of a successful love relationship entails the possession, or acquisition, of an adequate amount of physical, psychological, and spiritual knowledge paralleling, and in large measure the same as, that required for *good willing*. Thus *good will* and *good love* are closely related. As with good willing, the knowledge relevant to good loving concerns the structure of the human being, his various functions and the laws governing them; and general differential psychology in all its aspects (see Appendix Five, page 248).

After such a preparation, the specific tasks leading to the harmonization and unification of love and will can be undertaken most effectively. There are three effective methods suitable for this purpose:

—The first consists in developing the weaker of the two, making both loving and willing equally available.

—The second aims at awakening, and then manifesting, the higher aspects of both.

—The third is bringing them into operation together in alternation, in such a way that each arouses and reinforces the other.

1. The first task is to balance the love-will combination by increasing the proportion of the weaker function with respect to the stronger one. Emotional types, in whom love predominates, must see to the progressive development of the will and its increasingly active employment. Conversely, volitional types, those for whom the exercise of the will represents the line of least resistance, have to take particular care that the quality of love tempers and counterbalances its employment, rendering it harmless and constructive.

In the case of the will, the aim of the training is *the*

cultivation of aspects in which it may be deficient. This cultivation requires the elimination of the unwillingness to engage in active training. This unwillingness has its chief source in a basic inertia existing in all of us; but an antagonistic attitude toward the will can also be caused by the excessive reaction against its harsh and immoderate imposition in the past. The elimination of such antagonism can be accomplished, as I have previously mentioned, by recognizing and appreciating the *value* of, and the *need* for, an appropriate use of the will. The same can be said of love. Many people fear love, fear opening themselves to another human being, a group, or an ideal. Sincere and honest self-examination and self-analysis, or an analysis conducted with the help of others, are the means of discovering and unmasking, and then getting rid of, these resistances and fears.

2. The second method, that of awakening and then manifesting the *higher* aspects of both love and will, raises an important point of a general nature. Many of the limitations and errors of modern scientific psychology owe their origin to a failure (one might say unwillingness) to recognize that in both love and will there exist qualitative differences of level, degree, and value. Yet scientific psychology, while claiming to eliminate evaluations, has frequently (and indeed almost inevitably) formulated evaluations without being aware of it. As Maslow has said, "Science is based on human values and is itself a value system."

The existence of different levels of being having different values is an evident and undeniable manifestation of the great law of evolution, as it progresses from simple and crude stages to more refined and highly organized ones. Applying this to the sphere of love and disregarding here the question of the relationship between sexuality and love, it is evident that a love that is overpowering, possessive, jealous, and blind is at a lower level than one that is tender and concerned with the person of the loved one, that seeks his well-being and desires the union of the best aspects of both personalities. At still another level we find altruistic love, with its broad humanitarian perspective, animated by compassion and the urge to mitigate the sufferings and ills that beset humanity—the love called *caritas* or *agape*. How, then, can the differences in evolution, level, and value of the various kinds of love be ignored?

The same is equally true and evident in regard to the will, which, as we have seen, can at its lowest level be hard, egotistical, bent toward power and domination, ruthless and cruel. At higher levels, on the other hand, the will is directed toward objectives and purposes devoid of egotism and egocentric content. Animated by this kind of will, an individual tends to establish close relationships with other human beings, and will be ready to ally his will with that of others for constructive ends. As the basic human needs are being taken care of, the pull of what Maslow has termed the higher needs gradually emerges and asserts itself, and draws us toward ever greater expansions of consciousness and realization. This occurs not only in the spheres of love and will but also in the case of such functions as desire, imagination, and mental activity. We can deliberately choose to stimulate and foster this natural process of development and growth by means of skillful application of various techniques used in psychosynthesis, such as visualization, creative imagination, meditation, the "ideal model," transmutation and sublimation.

3. The third method aims at a gradual fusion of love and will and their resultant synergy. It forms an essential

part of psychosynthesis, the process whereby the multiplicity of tendencies, the autonomous, often conflicting elements, enter into an increasingly harmonious interaction culminating in their final fusion in the integrated human being.

All this, intentionally stated in simple terms as it is, seems elementary and obvious: yet anyone who sets himself to practice it soon realizes how difficult it is. In dealing with this subject, therefore, as with others in the course of this study, the use of expressions that are simple, easily understood, and as nontechnical as possible should not induce the reader to think that I consider these matters to be simple and easy to put into operation!

The gradual fusion of love and will is often characterized by periods of varying duration in which external circumstances or inner urges may occasion a temporary predominance of the normally weaker or less developed function. A simple case in point is that of a "volitional type" of man falling in love; another illustration is the manner in which a disaster, such as flood or earthquake, can arouse humanitarian feelings and a sense of human solidarity in an ordinarily self-centered and unfeeling individual. In a love type, the urge to fulfill his love arouses his will to the extent that he temporarily focuses his energies on the means leading him to reach the desired objective.

The Principle and Technique of Synthesis

If the various stages, qualities, and levels of the will, the corresponding ones of love, and the complex interactions between all of them are taken into account, as is indeed necessary, it will be apparent that the successful endeavor to achieve a synthesis between love and will demands much skill in action. It calls for persistent vigilance, for constant awareness from moment to moment. Various current spiritual movements and approaches rightly emphasize it and it has been widely practiced in the East.

But this awareness, this attitude of maintaining a conscious inner "presence," does not stop with the observation of what "happens" within oneself and in the external world. It makes possible the *active intervention* and *commitment* on the part of the self, who is not only an observer, but also a *will-er*, a *directing agent* of the play of the various functions and energies. This can be done by utilizing the principle of self-identification (see the exercise of identification in Appendix One, page 213). From the vantage point of the self, it is not a *compromise* between love and will which is being attempted, but a *synthesis*. The two elements are absorbed into a higher unity endowed with qualities which transcend those of either. The difference between such synthesis and a mere compromise is fundamental. It is indicated for a number of different situations in the triangular diagrams on pages 102–103.

The synthesis between the stages, qualities, and levels of love and will needs to be effected in such ways. Future research outlined in the Will Project (see Part III) should aim at ascertaining, through experiments, how these particular syntheses can be best brought about. Active watchfulness and direction of this kind demand the application of *wisdom*.

Like the will, wisdom is little in fashion today. Most people's idea of a sage is static, picturing someone aloof and far removed from so-called "reality" and life. One of psychology's tasks should be the rehabilitation of wisdom, by putting forward a truer conception of its vital, dynamic, and creative nature. This image of wisdom has

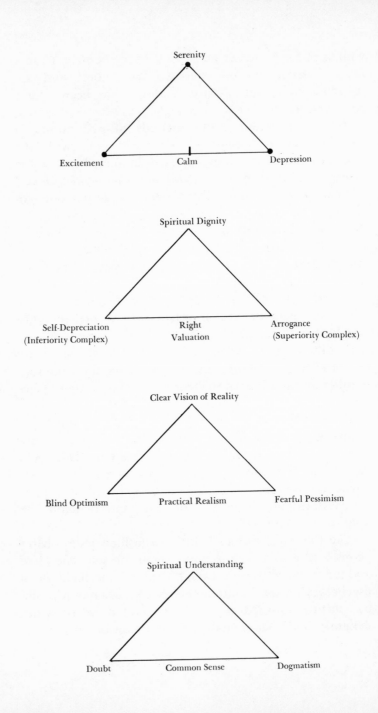

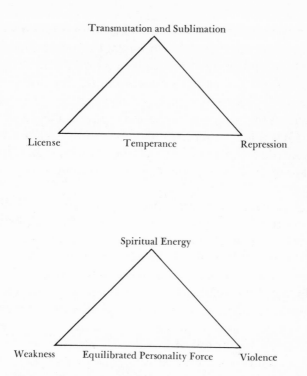

been arrestingly presented by Hermann Keyserling in *The Recovery of Truth*:

> The Chinese, who know more of wisdom than any other race, designate the wise by the combination of the ideographs for wind and lightning; wise, with them, is not the serene old man bereft of all illusions, but he who, like the wind, rushes headlong and irresistibly on his way and cannot be stopped nor laid hold of at any station of his career; who purifies the air in the manner of lightning, and strikes when there is need for it.

Paradoxical as it may sound, the self must use the *wise will* to synthesize the various stages of love and will. This process can be carried out because an essential attribute of wisdom is the power to "play with opposites," to regulate the interaction of antipodal forces and functions, thereby establishing a dynamic equalibrium and synthesis, without resorting to compromise, but rather by regulation *from a higher level*. This general process is described in my article "The Balancing and Synthesis of the Opposites." Here a few examples can serve to demonstrate the operation of the wise will in various situations and help point toward the union of love and will.

The polarity between "mind" and "heart," between reason and feeling (*Logos* and *Eros*), is regulated, first, by the recognition of their respective functions and of the legitimate field of action belonging to each of the two functions, so that neither dominates the other. This can be followed by a mutual and increasing cooperation and interpenetration between the two, finally arriving at the synthesis so well expressed by Dante in the words "intellectual light full of love."

The polarity between sensitivity and receptivity (*Pathos*), and dynamism or affirmativeness (*Ethos*), which, in a wider sense, corresponds to the psychosexual polarity— for the former role is the "feminine" and the latter the "masculine" modality—can also at first be controlled by a balanced adjustment, to be superseded by a creative synthesis.

The fundamental polarity between the human personality as a whole and the Transpersonal Self can also be resolved into a unity. This is the aim of a long process of transmutation, involving a protracted series of conflicts, approaches, and contacts, each producing a partial or more expanded fusion: in short, a process of transpersonal psychosynthesis. This constitutes the high effort, the central drama of man, who, either consciously or unconsciously, aspires to this goal, or is pushed toward it by his inability to find lasting satisfaction or a true peace until he has attained it. The phases and methods of such a fusion and synthesis have been described, in a preliminary way, in *Psychosynthesis*.

These various equilibrations, adjustments, and integrations can be produced in different ways. In a number of cases they are preceded by intense crises and conflicts. At other times they are reached in a more harmonious way by means of a gradual decrease in the oscillations of the "pendulum" which swings between the two extremes. A clear understanding of this process of psychosynthesis enables one to actively cooperate with it, and achieve it more easily and rapidly. The essential requirement, as previously mentioned, is to avoid identifying oneself with either of the two opposite poles, and to control, transmute, and direct their energies from a higher unifying center of awareness and power.

9

THE TRANSPERSONAL WILL

The recent development of the field of transpersonal psychology provides a good foundation and a convenient framework for dealing with the subject of the Transpersonal Will.

Maslow has clearly described the "hierarchy of needs" in *Motivation and Personality*. He speaks first of the basic psychological needs; then of the personal needs such as belonging and love, esteem, and self-actualization; and also of a third group: Transpersonal or Meta-needs. Achieving the satisfaction of the first two groups of needs often engenders, paradoxically, a sense of boredom, ennui, emptiness, and meaninglessness. It leads to a more or less blind search for "something other," something more. This is seen in many who, having had great satisfactions and successes in the ordinary world, become increasingly restless, rebellious, or depressed. Viktor Frankl has dealt extensively with this condition, which he has aptly termed "the existential vacuum":

Ever more patients complain of what they call an "inner void," and that is the reason why I have termed this "existential vacuum."

In contradistinction of the peak-experience so aptly described by Maslow, one could conceive of the existential vacuum in throes of an "abyss-experience."

But this condition need not necessarily be considered pathological. Frankl goes so far as to say, "The existential vacuum is no neurosis; or, if it is a neurosis at all, it is a sociogenic neurosis, or even a iatrogenic neurosis—that is to say, a neurosis which is caused by the doctor who pretends to cure it."

A striking example of intense existential vacuum (coexisting with perfect physical and mental health) is found in the *Confessions* of Leo Tolstoi. It is worth while to quote him in full.

So I lived; but five years ago something very strange began to happen to me. At first I experienced moments of perplexity and arrest of life, as though I did not know what to do or how to live, and I felt lost and became dejected. But this passed, and I went on living as before. Then these moments of perplexity began to recur oftener and oftener, and always in the same form. They were always expressed by the questions: What is it for? What does it lead to?

At first it seemed to me that these were aimless and irrelevant questions. I thought that it was all well known, and that if I should ever wish to deal with the solution it would not cost me much effort: just at present I had not time for it, but when I wanted to I should be able to find the answer. The questions however began to repeat themselves frequently, and to demand replies more and more insistently; and like drops of ink always falling on one place they ran together into one black blot.

Then occurred what happens to everyone sickening with a mortal internal disease. At first trivial signs of indisposition appear to which the sick man pays no attention; then these signs reappear more and more often and merge into one uninterrupted period of suffering. The suffering increases and, before the sick man can look round, what he took for a mere indisposition has already become more important to him than anything else in the world—it is death!

That was what happened to me. I understood that it was no casual indisposition but something very important, and that if these questions constantly repeated themselves they would have to be answered. And I tried to answer them. The questions seemed such stupid, simple childish ones; but as soon as I touched them and tried to solve them I at once became convinced, first, that they are not childish and stupid but the most important and profound of life's questions; and secondly that, try as I would, I could not solve them. Before occupying myself with my Samara estate, the education of my son, or the writing of a book, I had to know why I was doing it. As long as I did not know why, I could do nothing and could not live. Amid the thoughts of estate management which greatly occupied me at that time, the question would suddenly occur: "Well, you will have 6,000 desytinas of land in Samara Government and 300 horses, and what then?" . . . And I was quite disconcerted and did not know what to think. Or when considering plans for the education of my children, I would say to myself: "What for?" Or when considering how the peasants might become prosperous, I would suddenly say to myself: "But what does it matter to me?" Or when thinking of the fame my works would bring me, I would say to myself, "Very well; you will be more famous than Gogol or Pushkin or Shakespeare or Molière, or than all the writers in the world—and what of it?" And I could find no reply at all. The questions would not wait, they had to be answered at once, and if I did not answer them it was impossible to live. But there was no answer.

I felt that what I had been standing on had collapsed and that I had nothing left under my feet. What I had lived on no longer existed, and there was nothing left.

My life came to a standstill. I could breathe, eat, drink, and sleep, and I could not help doing these things; but there was no life, for there were no wishes the fulfilment of which I could consider reasonable. If I desired anything, I knew in advance that whether I satisfied my desire or not, nothing would come of it. Had a fairy come and offered to fulfil my desires I should not have known what to ask. If in moments of intoxication I felt something which, though not a wish, was a habit left by former wishes, in sober moments I knew this to be a delusion and that there was really nothing to wish for.

It had come to this, that I, a healthy, fortunate man, felt I could not longer live: some irresistible power impelled me to rid myself one way or other of life. I cannot say I wished to kill myself. The power which drew me away from life was stronger, fuller, and more widespread than any mere wish. It was a force similar to the former striving to live, only in a contrary direction. All my strength drew me away from life. The thought of self-destruction now came to me as naturally as thoughts of how to improve my life had come formerly.

And all this befell me at a time when all around me I had what is considered complete good fortune. I was not yet fifty; I had a good wife who loved me and whom I loved, good children, and a large estate which without much effort on my part improved and increased. I was respected by my relations and acquaintances more than at any previous time. I was praised by others and without much self-deception could consider that my name was famous. And far from being insane or mentally diseased, I enjoyed on the contrary a strength of mind and body such as I have seldom met with among men of my kind; physically I could keep up with the peasants at mowing, and mentally I could work for eight and ten hours at a stretch without experiencing any ill results from such exertion.

Tolstoi's statement is significant because it shows the fundamental importance of the *need for understanding the meaning of life.* Frankl in his book *Man's Search for Meaning* gives ample testimony of this. While a prisoner in Nazi concentration camps, he noticed that those who saw meaning in life, or who gave it meaning, demonstrated a surprising degree of strength and resistance. Finding this meaning proved to be of decisive survival value, as many of those who lacked such incentive gave up and died.

There is also a somewhat different type of crisis, the sense of *personal* futility. Here the individual feels that *he* is useless, that *his* life can have no point, or value, and can lead nowhere. This in my opinion is a delusion, because every form of existence *has* its place in the whole. The old story of the three stone-cutters illustrates the value of this realization. When a medieval cathedral was being built and three stone-cutters were asked in turn, "What are you doing?" the first replied in an angry tone, "As you see, I am cutting stones." The second answered, "I am earning a life for myself and my family." But the third said joyously, "I am building a great cathedral." All were doing exactly the same thing, but while the first had a sense of futility because of the dull and humble nature of his work, and the second found a small personal purpose in it, the third saw the real purpose of the stone-cutting. He realized that without it the cathedral could not be built, and he was infused with the *joy* of his partnership in a meaningful goal.

To help understand the dissatisfaction with "normal" life, we can look again at the diagram of the psychological constitution of man, found on page 14. The basic and normal personal needs concern the levels of the lower and middle psychological life, both conscious and unconscious. However, there is also a third and higher level—the area of the superconscious, which culminates in the Transpersonal Self.

It is both the drama and glory of man that this higher level, most often latent, sooner or later demands satisfaction; it demands to be taken into account and lived. There is a striking statement by Jung on this fact:

> To be "normal" is a splendid ideal for the unsuccessful, for all those who have not yet found an adaptation. But for people who have far more ability than the average, for whom it was never hard to gain successes and to accomplish their share of the world's work—for them restriction to the normal signifies the bed of Procrustes, unbearable boredom, infernal sterility and hopelessness. As a consequence there are many people who become neurotic because they are only normal, as there are people who are neurotic because they cannot become normal.

All needs evoke corresponding drives toward their satisfaction. The drives concerning the basic elementary needs are more or less blind, instinctive, and unconscious. But for the more personal needs the drives gradually lead to conscious volitional acts, aiming at their satisfaction. Therefore every need arouses, sooner or later, a corresponding *will*.

One might say the highest and fullest example of the *will to meaning* is found in the life of Gautama Buddha. When he realized what suffering there was in human life, he could have no peace; he started an intensive search for the causes of the suffering and the ways to eliminate it. For many years he tried different methods, including strict asceticism, but with no success. Finally, through persistence in meditation, one night under the famous Bodhi tree he achieved illumination. He "saw" in a flash of light all the mechanisms, the chain of causes, which produce the suffering and bondage of humanity; what he called the "wheel of causation." And then he saw also the way to break this chain and achieve freedom. He found meaning and the solution of life's problems through illumination. He blazed a trail and showed a way for others to follow.

But this illumination was the result and the reward of his *willed* endeavor. As D. T. Suzuki describes it:

> The most important fact that lies behind the experience of Enlightenment, therefore, is that the Buddha made the most strenuous attempt to solve the problem of ignorance and his utmost will-power was brought forth to bear upon a successful issue of the struggle. . . . Enlightenment therefore must involve the *will as well as the intellect.* It is an act of intuition born of the will. . . . The Buddha attained this end when a new insight came upon him at the end of his ever-circulatory reasoning from decay and death. . . . But he had an indomitable will; he wanted, with the utmost efforts of his will, to get into the very truth of the matter; he knocked and knocked until the doors of Ignorance gave way; and they burst open to a new vista never before presented to his intellectual vision.

The basic *need for meaning* has been stated in a concise and forceful way by Albert Einstein: "The man who regards his life as meaningless is not merely unhappy but hardly fit to live."

As a result of dissatisfaction with what is experienced as the meaninglessness of the present way of living—both personal and social—many feel a strong urge to evade it. In obeying this urge, they may try to reach beyond the limitations of ordinary consciousness and attain more expanded and intense states of awareness. Unfortunately many, often with the best intentions, try to attain these states through harmful, even destructive means. Therefore, it is necessary to realize clearly that there are two different, and in a sense opposite, ways for dealing with the existential anxiety. One is the attempt to escape it by returning to a primitive state of consciousness, to be reabsorbed into the "mother," into a prenatal state, to lose oneself in the collective life. This is the way of *regression*. The other is the above-mentioned way of *transcendence*, of "rising above" ordinary consciousness. Maslow has called these two conditions the "low nirvana" and the "high nirvana." The first, while it may give a temporary sense of release, and may show that there are states of expanded consciousness, cannot bring permanent satisfaction and does not offer a real and lasting solution. It only postpones the crisis, which will eventually reappear in exacerbated form. So we need to face courageously and willingly the requirements for transcending *the limitations* of personal consciousness, without losing the center of individual awareness. This is possible because individuality and universality are not mutually exclusive; they can be united in a blissful synthetic realization. At this point it might be objected that there have been many instances of *spontaneous*, sudden, unexpected illumination, without any previous conscious striving or exertion. In these cases the initiative is taken by the Transpersonal Self, which exerts a "pull" from above. This fact can be understood by considering the psychological constitution of human beings. We have seen that the will is the function in closest relation to the self, the most direct expression of the self. This is true both for the personal self and for the Transpersonal Self. Just as there is a personal will—the one we have been considering up to now—so there is a Transpersonal Will, which is an expression of the Transpersonal Self and operates from the superconscious levels of the psyche. It is its action which is felt by the personal self, or "I," as a "pull" or "call."

The existence and the "presence" of this transcendent

Reality or Self has been interestingly asserted by Jung in the inscription over the door of his house at Kussnacht: *"Vocatus, sive non vocatus, Deus aderit"* ("God will be present whether called in or not"). And this experience has been reported by many, often interpreted as a call from God or some higher being. I shall not discuss the interpretation here, but the reality and the nature of this process should be recognized.

Experiences of spontaneous illumination have been reported by many, and many of these experiences are detailed in R. M. Bucke's *Cosmic Consciousness*, and William James's *The Varieties of Religious Experience*. Both these pioneering books contain much valuable material, and the interpretations given by both authors are still pertinent to a considerable extent. A collection of firsthand reports of spontaneous illuminations occurring to "ordinary" people is contained in Winslow Hall's *Observed Illuminates*.

Accounts of religious experiences often speak of a "call" from God, or a "pull" from some Higher Power; this sometimes starts a "dialogue" between the man and this "Higher Source," in which each alternately invokes and evokes the other. In other cases the pull from "above" takes the form of an imperative demand, which may even be felt temporarily as a persecution. This has been vividly expressed by Francis Thompson in his poem "The Hound of Heaven." These are the opening stanzas:

> I fled Him, down the nights and down the days;
> I fled Him, down the arches of the years;
> I fled Him, down the labyrinthine ways
> Of my own mind, and in the mist of tears
> I hid from Him, and under running laughter.
>   Up vistaed hopes I sped;

And shot, precipitated,
Adown Titanic glooms of chasmed fears,
From those strong Feet that followed, followed after,
     But with unhurrying chase,
     And unperturbed pace,
Deliberate speed, majestic instancy,
     They beat—and a Voice beat
     More instant than the Feet—
"All things betray thee, who betrayest me."

A good description of the "call" of a Higher Principle has been given, once again, by Jung:

> What, in the last analysis, induces a man to choose his own way and so climb out of unconscious identity with the mass as out of a fog bank. . . . It is what is called "vocation." . . . Who has vocation hears the voice of the inner man; he is *called* . . . a historic case is the "daimon" of Socrates. . . . To have vocation means in the original sense *to be addressed by a voice*. We find the clearest examples of this in the Confessions of the Old Testament Prophets. Nor is this merely an ancient manner of speech, as is shown by the confessions of historic personalities such as Goethe and Napoleon, to mention two familiar examples, who made no secret of their feeling of vocation. Now, vocation, or the feeling of vocation, is not perchance the prerogative of great personalities, but also belongs to the small ones. . . .

It should be noted, however, that when the Transpersonal Will becomes active, many diverse effects can result from the interplay between it and the often rebellious will of the personal self. I have discussed the stages of the crisis produced and ways to deal with them in the second chapter of *Psychosynthesis*.

The aspiration and will of the personal self and the pull from the Transpersonal Self to transcend the limitations of "normal" consciousness and life do not manifest themselves only as a search and will to meaning, to enlightenment. There are other types of transcendence which are experienced by the corresponding types of human beings. Some of the chief ones are:

1. Transcendence through transpersonal *love*.
2. Transcendence through transpersonal *action*.
3. Transcendence through *beauty*.
4. Transcendence through SELF-*realization*.

These ways of transcendence can also be expressed in terms of *will*, the fundamental *will to transcend personality limitations through union with someone or something greater and higher*. More exactly, in all of them we find the union of *will* and *love*.

I. Transcendence through Transpersonal Love

In *full human love* there is a transpersonal aspect. It can be defined as the relationship between the superconscious levels in both persons—a joint realization of Transpersonal Reality. It can be combined with love at all personality levels; thus there can be at times a combination of sexual, emotional, and transpersonal love. The perfect love could be considered as the union at all levels. The corresponding will can be called the *will to union through love*. One of the fullest depictions of this love has been given by Richard Wagner in *Tristan and Isolde*. The two personalities are included and transcended, and there is unification with the transcendent Reality through the union between the two.

A second kind of transcendence through love is through *altruistic love*. There is a difference here between personal good will, which I have mentioned earlier, and the Transpersonal Will of which altruistic love is an expression. It has been called *caritas* and *agape*; its highest and purest expression is *compassion*.

Altruistic love is not limited to the members of the human family. It can also embrace all living things in the animal and vegetable kingdoms of nature. This inclusiveness is expressed in the Buddhist love for all living creatures, and by Saint Francis in his "Song of the Creatures." One might say that an increasingly conscious sense of this universal brotherhood is behind the growing trend toward the cultivation of harmonious relations with the environment. This is the higher and broader aspect of ecology.

A third kind of transcendence through love is the aspiration to unity with the Supreme Being, generally called God or Universal Reality. It is the way of *mystical love*. The utterances of the great mystics often contain passionate references to this urge for union with God. And the greatest mystics have demonstrated a strong and well-developed will.

II. Transcendence through Transpersonal Action

The highest forms of humanitarian and social action have a transpersonal character. They are motivated by the Transpersonal Will, which is independent of, and at times even against, the personal will, against the instinct for self-preservation and the drive to personal self-assertion. These actions may involve courage, hardships, sacrifices, risks. They may be prompted by selfless devotion and active consecration to an ideal or a cause, and can reach the peaks of true heroism.

III. Transcendence through Beauty

Transpersonal realization through beauty can be called the *aesthetic way*. Beauty is felt as a *need* by many people, and the corresponding drive to beauty arouses therefore the *will to beauty*. There are two aspects of this will; there is the *contemplation* of beauty and the *creation* of beautiful things.

It is in the creation of beauty, however, that the *will* is more manifest. It is often realized that the artist is driven by the urge to create, that his personality is impelled by this urge which is sometimes easy and joyous, but more often is difficult and even painful. Often the personality rebels or tries to evade the higher urge. Yet the artist is *obliged* to create; he's given no peace until he has obeyed the urge to create that which has been prepared in the superconscious realm. Goethe seems to be speaking of himself and his own inner need to create when, in *Tasso*, he writes, "I've struggled day and night against this need. I'm worn out trying to shut up my breast. 'Tis useless! Sing I must: Else life's not life."

Thus, there is a direct connection between will and beauty. This is a fact not often realized because in many cases, at the personality level, artists may have little developed will, and more highly developed feelings, emotions, and imagination. It is often their Transpersonal Self which exercises its Will and compels the personality to express beauty. Yet there have been and there are artists who have clearly demonstrated personal will as well. An outstanding example of strong conscious will to create, persisting through old age, is Michelangelo. The hardships to which he submitted himself in painting the Sistine Chapel offer abundant proof. A more modern instance of a really heroic will to create is given by the French painter Renoir. In the last years of his life his hands were crippled with arthritis. Nevertheless he had the brush tied to his hand and with difficulty and great pain succeeded in continuing to paint until the end of his life. His personal will was in tune with his higher Will. Beethoven was deaf in his last years, yet he followed the urge to go on composing and wrote some of his finest compositions when he could not hear them. There are many such examples of artists who are disabled and yet succeed at creating by virtue of their indomitable wills.

IV. Transcendence through SELF-Realization

Following this way to transcendence can be said to be the outcome of the urge and the deliberate will to realize all human potentialities, especially the transcendent ones. This means giving particular value to those emerging potentialities which belong to the sphere of the superconscious, and have their origin in the Transpersonal Self.

It is therefore necessary to have a clear conception of the difference between SELF-realization and self-actualization. Maslow has pointed out this distinction in his paper "Theory Z." He says that besides the "merely healthy self-actualizers" there are also the "transcending self-actualizers"; transcending self-actualizers are *more* self-actualizing than normal self-actualizers because they are more fully involved with Being values—with SELF-realization. This is not the actualization of the potentialities latent in the "normal" human personality, but the progressive manifestation of *transcendent,* transpersonal potentialities, culminating with the direct experiential awareness of the Transpersonal SELF.

The well-rounded, integrated, self-actualizing personality can be quite selfish or at least self-centered. Self-actualization does not imply any higher motivation; it can be motivated by the drive to success and to displaying one's own individual powers. Not only can a self-actualized person be satisfied with himself, but he can even be antagonistic to any further growth. This has been well dealt with by Frank Haronian in his paper "Repression of the Sublime." Haronian asks, "Why do we evade . . . the challenge of personal growth? We fear growth because it means abandoning the familiar for the unknown, and that always involves risks." Haronian quotes Angyal and then Maslow on the same subject. Maslow speaks of the "Jonah Complex":

> In my own notes I had at first labelled this defense "the fear of one's own greatness" or "the evasion of one's destiny" or "the running away from one's own best talent." . . . It is certainly possible for most of us to be greater than we are in actuality. We all have unused potentialities or not fully developed ones. It is certainly true that many of us evade our constitutionally suggested vocations. . . . So often we run away from the responsibilities dictated (or rather suggested) by nature, by fate, even sometimes by accident, just as Jonah tried in vain to run away from *his* fate.

Maslow has presented an illuminating progression of five stages of evolutionary development. The types belonging to the first two stages are under Theory X. They are primarily determined by deficiency needs. The third and fourth types come under Theory Y. They are primarily determined by drives to self-actualization. The fifth type is under what he calls Theory Z. This is the person who aligns his life with transcending values. While emphasizing the value of the reaches of transpersonal self-realization, Maslow has wisely warned against making it something supernatural and separate from the other levels of actualization:

> Transcendence also means to become divine or godlike, to go beyond the merely human. But one must be careful here not to make anything extra-human or supernatural out of this kind of statement. I am thinking of using the word "metahuman" or

"B-human" in order to stress that this is part of human nature even though it is not often seen in fact. It is still a potentiality of human nature.

It should be made clear that "distinction" does not mean "separation." All these levels of development are distinct; however, while there are individuals in whom the transpersonal aspect, although present, is so completely latent as to be practically nonexistent, in many others the different levels of personal and transpersonal realization can be active in various proportions, and also in various degrees at different times. Thus, one can have achieved a certain measure of genuine transpersonal SELF-realization while not having complete self-actualization. This is in accord with what Maslow says in the second paragraph of "Theory Z": "It seems to me that I have found some degree of transcendence in many people other than self-actualizing ones." In the terminology of psychosynthesis, self-actualization corresponds to personal psychosynthesis. This includes the development and harmonizing of all human functions and potentialities at all levels of the lower and middle area in the diagram of the constitution of man. Instead, SELF-realization concerns the third higher level, that of the superconscious, and pertains to Transpersonal or spiritual psychosynthesis.

SELF-realization itself has three different stages. The first is the activation and expression of the potentialities residing in the superconscious: it includes the various types of transcendence previously mentioned. Leonardo da Vinci or Goethe would be good examples of this. The second stage of SELF-realization is the *direct awareness* of the SELF, which culminates in the unification of the consciousness of the personal self, or "I," with that of the

Transpersonal Self. Here one might mention those who have done self-sacrificing work for a beneficent cause in any field. Active humanitarians who have given themselves to a cause are good examples: Gandhi, Florence Nightingale, Martin Luther King, Schweitzer. Schweitzer is typical because he gave up even some of his higher interests—music and culture—in order to do humanitarian work. In terms of will, it is the unification of the personal will with the Transpersonal Will. The third stage of SELF-realization is the communion of the Transpersonal Self with the Universal Self, and correspondingly of the individual will with the Universal Will. Here we find the highest mystics of all times and places.

10

THE UNIVERSAL WILL

The question of the existence of a Universal Will and its relation to individual wills is fundamental because it is closely connected with the larger problem of the relation between man and the ultimate Universal Reality.

A difficulty in dealing with this subject is the fact that up until recently this relationship has been conceived and expressed chiefly in religious terms. At present such an approach has little appeal to many people, and is even flatly denied. One might say, in rather irreverent terms, that presently God has a bad press. Some have asserted in a sensational way that "God is dead"; but apart from that, for many people God is only an abstraction, a concept, a symbol, a matter of faith in the sense of more or less blind belief, or at the utmost, of hope—but not a living Reality. It does not affect their feelings and their actions. In practice, they live as if God did not exist.

This attitude can be understood largely as a reaction against both the anthropomorphic images of God and the theologies which have attempted to give theoretical conception to a Reality which transcends any such formulations. Man had created a god in his own image, attributing to him his own human qualities and often, more or less explicitly, his own limitations and imperfections. It is these images and the various theological models of God which are being refused, which are "dying."

There are other approaches to ultimate Reality, however, which are more satisfactory and fruitful. One is the *intuitional approach*. The intuition has been recognized by many, both in the East and in the West, as a true and higher means of cognition. It has been considered by Jung and others as a psychological function in its own right, as real and legitimate as any of the others. The difference can be said to consist between the attempts to "prove" the existence of God through intellectual and rational means—as has been attempted by certain schools of theology—and the intuitive, direct experience of communion with the ultimate Reality.

But there is another distinction which it would be well to make clear: the word "reason" has been used in two ways by philosophers. One employs "reason" to mean the mental, analytical concept of reason. This might be called Aristotelean. And it is the one adopted, more or less consciously, by modern science and by "rationalistic" philosophers. The other conception of reason corresponds to the *Logos* of Plato and the Transcendental Reason of Kant and others.

A second approach to reality is through the perception of analogies.* The approach of analogy is based on the

* The existence of analogies throughout nature is well known to science. It has led to several important technological developments, among which is the analog computer.

essential unity of all the aspects of Reality, from the smallest to the largest. Thus there is a close correspondence between the microcosm and the macrocosm in general, and specifically between man and the universe. But this basic identity of nature does not mean that man in his normal state of consciousness can *mentally* understand, "comprehend," the immense scope and meaning of the ultimate Reality. The following analogy of the relation between a drop of water and all the waters existing in our planet may help to clarify the point: if a drop had intelligence, it could assert that it had the same nature as all the waters of the planet; that is, the same chemical composition, two atoms of hydrogen and one of oxygen connected according to a certain pattern. All the waters on the planet have this same chemical composition. But there are among them numerous differences: differences of *location* (oceans, lakes, rivers), of *conditions* (liquid, solid, gas), of *functions* (water can be part of a vegetable, animal, or human organism), and of *relationships* with other substances (solutions). A tiny drop, if it had intelligence, could not conceive or even imagine all these things. But it would be aware at least that it had the same chemical composition as the rest.

Let us apply this analogy to man and the universe. Man can have the intuitive realization of his essential identity with the supreme Reality. In the East it has been expressed as the identity between the Atman and the Brahman. In the West some mystics have boldly proclaimed the identity between man and God. Others have emphasized that Life is One, that there is only One Life. But this does not mean that man's *mind* can grasp the wonder and mysteries of the cosmic manifestation. Only through a series of expansions of consciousness, only by reaching ever higher states of awareness, may he gradually experience *some* of those wondrous mysteries.

Of such transpersonal possibilities the most enlightened men and women of all ages have given testimony, expressing them in basically the same way, above the differences and colorings due to individual and cultural conditionings.

To reverse the anthropomorphic position, it can be said that all human qualities and functions are partial "reflections" in the etymological sense (as images in a mirror or light through a prism) of qualities and aspects of the transcendent Reality.

As we have seen, man's basic existential experience, when disidentified from all the various psychological elements, is the conscious "Being"—is *being a living self.* This is an aspect of the Universal SELF or Being. The experiential realization of this relationship has successive *degrees* which have been pictured on page 127.

In diagram one, the radiation of the "star" symbolizing the Transpersonal Self is directed almost completely within the periphery or area of the individual psyche, indicating that the attention of the SELF is directed chiefly toward the personal self, or "I," and its activity is bent on influencing the whole man by radiation from and through the superconscious level.

In the second diagram the attention and activity of the SELF are shown as evenly distributed between the downward direction toward the personality, and the upward direction toward the transcendent Reality. In this condition, achieved in and through many stages of expanded awareness, the subject has some realization of his participation in a universal state of Being, while preserving at the same time a vivid, even sharpened,

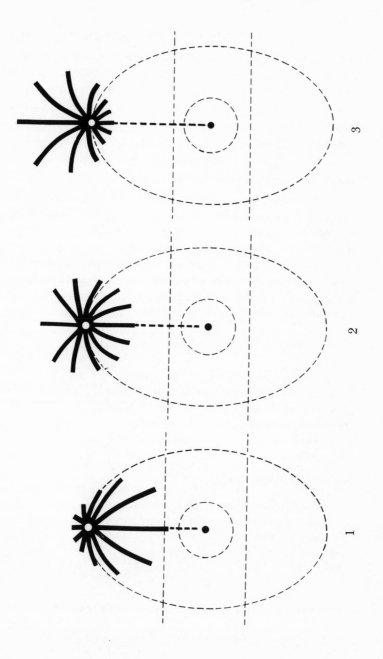

1   2   3

sense of individual identity, of being fully "himself."

The radiation of the star in the third diagram indicates the highest states of transcendence, in which the sense of individual identity is dimmed and may even seem temporarily lost. These are the states variously called *samadhi, prajna, satori,* ecstasies, cosmic consciousness, etc.

But even in these states the sense of individuality is not *wholly* lost. This has been clearly formulated by Lama Anagarika Govinda in the following way:

> Individuality is not only the necessary and complementary opposite of universality, but the focal point through which alone universality can be experienced. The suppression of individuality, the philosophical or religious denial of its value or importance, can only lead to a state of complete indifference and dissolution, which may be a liberation from suffering but a purely negative one, as it deprives us of the highest experience towards which the process of individuation seems to aim: the experience of perfect enlightenment, of Buddhahood, in which the universality of our true being is realized.
>
> Merely to "merge into the whole" like the "drop into the sea," without having realized that wholeness, is only a poetical way of accepting annihilation and evading the problem that the fact of our individuality poses. Why should the universe evolve individualized forms of life and consciousness if this were not consistent with or inherent in the very spirit or nature of the universe?

and by Radhakrishnan:

> The peculiar privilege of the human self is that he can consciously join and work for the whole and embody in his own life the purpose of the whole. . . . The two elements of selfhood: uniqueness (each-ness), and universality (all-ness), grow together until at last the most unique becomes the most universal.

Maslow describes this experience, in his article "Various Meanings of Transcendence," as follows:

> Also useful would be Bucke's use of cosmic consciousness. This is a special phenomenological state in which the person somehow perceives the whole cosmos or at least the unity and integration of it and of everything in it, including his Self. He then feels as if he belongs by right in the cosmos. He becomes one of the family rather than an orphan. He comes inside rather than being outside looking in. He feels simultaneously small because of the vastness of the universe, but also an important being because he is there in it by absolute right. He is a part of the universe rather than a stranger to it or an intruder in it.

The existence of a universal mind, of an inherent rationality of the Universe, has been affirmed by many in various ways, both philosophical and scientific. A discussion of the validity of these conceptions cannot be made here—it would lead too far. But in a general way a similar analogy can be made for all human functions. All human *love*, even in its highest transpersonal aspect, can be considered as the partial expression of a universal principle of *LOVE*. The mystics of all times and places have testified to having experienced the reality of such love. The physical manifestation of love offers an evident analogy with, and can be considered as a reflection of, the universal polarity, the interplay between what has been variously called spirit-matter; Yang-Yin; Shiva-Shakti, etc.*

The same relationship of analogy exists between the

---

* All that has been said concerns only *Reality in manifestation*, or in the process of manifesting, where there are *degrees* of transcendence. Of the *unmanifest*, or transcendent Reality in an *absolute* sense nothing can be said. It can be indicated or hinted at only through negations: not-this, not-that, no-thing, the "Void." This aspect of Reality has been emphasized by some schools of Northern Buddhism and in the West by Meister Eckhart. An extensive discussion of this subject from different angles by various authors is contained in the journal *Hermes*, 6, "Le Vide," edited by J. Matsui, Minard, Paris, 1969.

individual will and the Universal Will. It is based on the intimate relation which, as we have seen, exists between the self and the will at all levels. This relationship has been affirmed to be an existential reality by those who have experienced it. Here again let us recognize that if there was not a Universal Will, man would possess something not existing in the universe, and therefore the microcosm would be superior to the macrocosm—indeed a ridiculous conceit!

The harmonization, communion, unification, and fusion of the two wills has been—and is—the deep aspiration and, one might say, the highest, even if often unrealized, *need* of humanity. It has been felt and expressed in various ways according to the various concepts of Reality held by the different types of human beings. Essentially, it means tuning in and willingly participating in the rhythms of Universal Life. In Indian philosophy, this is called *sattva,* the *guna* of rhythm and of harmonious response to divine urge. The Chinese call this attitude *wu-wei,* or identification with the *tao.* For the Stoics and Spinoza it has been the willing acceptance of one's "destiny." For those having a devotional nature or a religious conception of faith, it is the relationship and eventual unification of man's will with God's will.

Many descriptions and testimonies of this relationship, and of the vicissitudes of its interplay, of the conflicts and the culminating of the two wills, can be found in the writings of the greatest mystics, of both the East and the West. Here I shall quote only the poetic expression given to it by Dante in the closing verses of the *Divine Comedy*:

> But, rolling like a wheel that never jars,
> My will and wish were now by love impelled,
> The love that moves the sun and all the other stars.

The most direct and highest statement of the will-to-unification has been made by Christ: "Not my will, but thine be done," and its achievement is in His triumphant affirmation, "I and the Father are one."

Part Two
The Stages
of Willing

11

FROM INTENTION
TO REALIZATION

The highest level of the will, its fusion with the Universal Will Itself, is the very apex of our journey: we have glimpsed the culmination and perfection of the will. But to best begin the effective training of the will for its progressive ascent through the attainment of strength, skill, goodness, and universality, we must now proceed to an examination of the *act* of the will itself.

The act of will consists of six sequential phases or stages. They are:

1. *The Purpose, Aim, or Goal, based on Evaluation, Motivation, and Intention.*
2. *Deliberation.*
3. *Choice and Decision.*
4. *Affirmation: the Command, or "Fiat," of the Will.*
5. *Planning and Working Out a Program.*
6. *Direction of the Execution.*

These six stages are like the links in a chain; therefore the chain itself—that is, the act of willing—is only as strong as its weakest link. So the performance of an act of will is going to be more or less successful and effective according to how successfully and effectively each of the stages is carried out. Let me note, however, that we are dealing here with the act of will in its ideal and complete state: not as a facsimile of every willed act but rather as a guide to complete, purposive action. While important acts of will warrant a careful consideration and the step-by-step execution of each stage, in many practical cases sometimes one, sometimes another stage will be central, will call for the greatest time and effort. Other stages might be completely satisfactory with a minimum of effort and attention.

For example, the head of a foundation with grant money to give to good causes may spend considerable time and effort to clarify in his mind what his *goals* are. He would then laboriously *deliberate* on the many possibilities, weighing the advantages and disadvantages of proposals that come to him. Eventually he will *choose* one and with little further effort *decide* to fund it. Then, as he has done many times before, he will *plan* to ask his secretary to notify the recipient, and will *direct* that a check be made to him. Here the first two stages are quite prominent; decision less so; affirmation may be hard to perceive, while the planning consisted simply in relying on the services of his secretary; and the direction of the execution was limited to having his secretary notify and pay the recipient.

At noon, the same man may shift his *aim* to having lunch. He will quickly *deliberate* on the various possibilities, *choose* one among several nearby restaurants, and *decide* to go there. Perhaps he may meet a friend on the

way and chat with him. After a while, if the acquaintance leaves, he may remember that before getting
sidetracked he had decided to go to the restaurant. So he
affirms to himself that he will now proceed without
allowing himself to be further interrupted. He rapidly
plans the road to follow, and gets on his way.

That evening he may have some friends for dinner,
and (let's say he is a gourmet cook) may want to cook a
meal for them. He quickly *deliberates* and *decides* what
meal to prepare, *affirms* to himself that he will produce
the best of which he is capable, then spends considerable
time *planning* how to prepare the ingredients and how to
cook the various dishes. Later he proceeds to the actual
execution, drawing to a large extent on habit patterns
and memories from his previous experience, but remaining *watchful* that his almost automatic activity
carefully follows his plans as far as sequence, accuracy of
the recipes, etc.

So while not every stage of the will may be important
in any one willed act, we need to be proficient in *all* the
stages in order to act effectively in different circumstances. It has been my observation—and one easy to
confirm—that the principal cause of failure in complet-
ing an act of will is that people often have difficulty
carrying out one or another specific stage: in other words,
they get stuck at a particular point in the sequence.
Therefore, understanding the various stages and their
functions is most valuable in uncovering the specific weak
point, or points, in which one needs to become more
proficient; in selecting the most suitable approaches and
techniques to do so; and, even more important, in
realizing the far-reaching over-all benefits that can be
derived from such work. Just as in personal psychosynthesis the harmonizing of the personality functions requires

the strengthening of the ones which are underdeveloped, so to acquire a fully effective will we need to know how to will *completely*, how to carry the act of volition successfully from its inception through its culmination, without getting lost somewhere along the way.

In order to give a general view of the subject, here is a brief description of each of the six functional stages of the will in action.

1. *The aim, or goal:* The chief characteristic of the volitional act is the existence of a *purpose* to be achieved; the clear vision of an aim, or goal, to be reached. But while this is indeed an indispensable characteristic, it is in itself not sufficient. In fact, so long as this vision of the goal remains in the realm of the imagination, or contemplation, it is not as yet will *in action*. First, the aim must be *valuated* and *assessed;* then it must arouse *motives* which generate the *urge* and the *intention* to achieve it. The word "motive" itself indicates something active, dynamic. Motives are aroused by the *values* that we attach to the goals we seek to attain.

2. But this alone is not enough. Many possible goals exist. We certainly cannot attain them all singly, and much less so all at the same time. Therefore, a *choice* has to be made. In order to make such a choice we must determine which, among the many possible goals, is *preferable*. Determining this is the function of *deliberation,* in which the various goals, our possibilities for realizing them, the desirability and the consequences of doing so, and all other relevant factors must be kept in mind and examined.

3. Deliberation must be followed by *choice* and a consequent *decision*. This means the choice of a given aim and the setting aside or discarding of others.

4. The choice and decision must be confirmed by an

affirmation. This activates and fosters the dynamic and creative energies needed to ensure the achievement of the goal.

5. After that, a careful elaboration of a *plan* and *program* is needed. These are based on the consideration and selection of the various *means* and *phases* of the execution of the plan through time and according to circumstances, conditions, and existing possibilities.

6. Finally comes the *direction of the execution.* This is a specific task of the will, the proper function of which is *not* to carry out the execution *directly,* as is commonly supposed. The will can and should make skillful use of the other psychological and bodily functions and energies existing in the personality: thinking and imagination, perceptions and intuition, feelings and impulses, as well as the physical organs of action. To employ an analogy from the theater, the will is the director of the entire production but normally he is not himself one of the actors.

This direction must also include constant *supervision* of the execution. The will at first calls up, or musters, the various functions needed for its purpose and gives them definite instructions, directions, commands. But the will must also supervise their activities, watch the development of the program, see to it that it follows the right course. This entails, as we shall see, a firm *subordination* of the various means to the underlying purpose and a constant *adaptation* of their use to changing conditions and circumstances.

12

PURPOSE, EVALUATION, MOTIVATION, INTENTION

In the heading of this stage, four elements have been grouped because they are interrelated in such a way that they should not be treated as different stages. In fact, a *purpose* is the will to reach a goal, an objective; but a goal is not such if it is not regarded as *valuable*. Similarly, a motive is not a motive if it does not "move," if it does not impel toward a goal. And the direction of the motive is given by *intention*.

Moreover, these aspects do not always succeed each other in a fixed order. Sometimes a *motive* or an *intention* appears first to the consciousness, for example, a prompting toward some ideal not yet clear or defined. Or one becomes aware of a moral, social, aesthetic, or religious *value*, which only later becomes connected to an aim, a specific goal to be achieved. At other times the vision comes first, the intuitive flash, the illumination that reveals a *goal* or a task to which a *value* is then attributed; and this arouses the *motives* which urge toward actualization and the *intention* to achieve it. Thus there can be a variety of dynamic relationships among purpose, evaluation, motive, and intention.

Another way of indicating these relationships is as follows: motives and intentions are based on evaluations; evaluations are based on the *meaning* attributed to life. But this meaning, in its turn, is given by the aim or purpose of life itself, and by its achievement. Therefore it is very helpful for putting the will into operation to have a positive conception of the meaning and purpose of life; to admit, first of all, that life *has* a purpose which is meaningful; second, that this purpose is positive, constructive, valuable—in one word, that it is *good.*

Of this we can become aware through self-observation, or introspection. But when we come to a closer study of *motivation,* things become much more complicated. Psychoanalysis has laid great emphasis upon the fact that unconscious motivations exist, and that often we act in the belief that we do so from a given conscious motive when in reality we are also, or principally, impelled by drives of which we are not aware. These overcome the censorship of the ego by means of rationalization. But even before psychoanalysis, attention had been called to the human tendency to find apparently good justifications for actions that are not good; justifications to ourselves and justifications to others. This tendency could be compared to the pleading of an inner attorney who defends the cause of the more intense urges operating in the unconscious.

In this connection, we can see one of those reactions or extreme oscillations that appear frequently in life. Classical psychology took account only of conscious motivations. Then, by contrast, psychoanalysis concerned itself only, or almost only, with unconscious motivations and urges, thus arriving, for all practical purposes, at the negation of the will.

It may be said that, as in many other cases, the truth lies in the middle. There are conscious motivations and unconscious motivations; or rather one might say more accurately that there is almost always a combination of the two, in very variable proportions. Thus an accurate analysis is required for using the will function with true awareness: either a self-analysis or an analysis by a therapist or an educator, according to the case.

This occasion does not permit my dwelling on the techniques of this analysis. I will simply point out an error into which we very often fall when we become aware of the motives within us. In Chapter 6, "Practical Applications of the Skillful Will," I have recommended the technique of "acting as if"; that is, of acting as if a psychological attitude existed in us, instead of the contrary one. Some are shocked at the use of this method because they consider it hypocritical; they say in effect: "If I am angry and harbor resentment against someone, for whatever reason, good or bad, and if I treat him with kindness and smiles, I am not being authentic—true to myself." But in reality it is not a question of hypocrisy. *This is due to the psychological multiplicity that exists in each of us.* "Acting as if" would be hypocritical *if* we did so with the purpose of deceiving others for selfish ends, or if we deceived ourselves into believing that our lower motives do not exist. But if, when an impulse or motive of hostility and resentment against someone arises in us, *we,* our true, our genuine self, do not approve of it and refuse to identify with it, then our *real will* is to choose the better motive and to act benevolently *in spite of* the impulse that urges us to treat the person badly. We can *choose* the motive to which we give free course.

Generally, opposite motives or urges in us tend to neutralize one another, and our task consists in intensifying the "potential" of the energies of good will and understanding so that they not only neutralize the hostile drives, but are stronger than they. Here, however, a reservation should be made, lest we fall into the Victorian trap of being repressive and thus suffer from the reactions of suppressed or repressed energies. Should, for example, the hostile tendencies be very intense, "acting as if" is not sufficient and, if used prematurely, can provoke undesirable results. In these cases, the methods of harmless "discharge" (catharsis) and of transmutation and sublimation should first be employed. In saying this I am not recommending that one *never* be aggressive or that one never fight; I mean that one has the freedom of *choice* about whether, and *to what extent,* to give direct expression to the impulse or motive, even if it be one of deeply felt anger or hurt. Furthermore, in making this choice, this decision, we can make use of the resources of clear understanding as well as of the guidance of the Transpersonal Self. The point is that choices and decisions are possible. The act of will and intention then involves a decision to accept or not accept an impulse. Authenticity does not consist in giving in to a bad motive simply because it exists.

Considered in this light, to behave in a benevolent manner even though one feels an impulse of anger can be the highest form of sincerity, for it corresponds to what we *would wish to be completely,* and *already are partially.* Such a recognition eliminates the misunderstanding about authenticity. Many, in fact, behave badly and excuse themselves on the score of being authentic. But this is often the authenticity of the cave man. The method of "acting as if" we possessed the desired feelings is neither sham nor hypocrisy. It is an effective way of becoming more and more what we wish we could be continuously. *We are,* essentially and genuinely, *what we will to be,* even if we often fail to manifest it.

In considering motivations, then, one is helped by distinguishing between two classes which we may designate respectively as *drives* and *urges,* and *reasons. Drives* and *urges* can be conscious or unconscious and can be generically regarded as spontaneous tendencies which "move" us or tend to do so. *Reasons,* on the other hand, to be really such, must be conscious and have a cognitive, mental aspect. They presuppose a clear vision of the goal, a recognition of its value, and the intention to reach it. One can take a drive or urge, test its rationality, and transform it into a reason.

If we look more closely at the evaluation of motivations, we see that frequently they cannot be labeled simply "good" or "bad." Honest observation, first of all of ourselves and then of others, frequently reveals that the motives and reasons that determine actions are *multiple* and of various kinds; a mixture of selfish and altruistic motives is frequent. Those whose approach is exclusively psychoanalytical maintain that the "real" motives are the instinctual and lower ones, and that the others are simply a cloak, or rationalization, of them. At the other extreme, the rigid and uncompromising idealists demand for themselves and for others an absolute purity of intention and condemn every motive that does not meet this criterion. But the existence of lower motives (let us designate them thus merely for simplicity of language) does not exclude the coexistence and *genuineness* of higher motives. The fundamental multiplicity of the human being, and of his being aware, and therefore acting, *on* and *from* different levels guarantees a multiplicity of motives, all of which are equally "real," genuine, and authentic. The nature of psychological conflicts can be explained in these terms; many of them could be said to be conflicts between various levels of intentions and motives.

But there is another interesting fact: the reasons and motives of different levels are not always in conflict. Often not only do they coexist peacefully but they also converge toward the same goal, and participate in, and thus cooperate in, executing the same volitional act. An interpretation of the paradoxical Talmudic saying "Serve God both with your bad impulses and with your good impulses" becomes possible. In modern psychological language, we might say that such service is equivalent to directing all the biopsychological tendencies to higher purposes and creative activities.

To do so presents a number of advantages. The first is the avoidance of the condemnation and repression into the unconscious of the "lower" drives, or the forestalling of a depressing guilt feeling and the harmful consequences arising from it. The knowledge of the existence of these "lower" elements in ourselves need neither surprise nor depress us; they exist in all human beings! Everyone is a little world, a microcosm in which all the kingdoms of nature are represented: the mineral, in bones, etc; the vegetative life; the animal instincts; then the "human conditions," from primitive man to the highest human possibilities. At the present time we represent the sum of all the evolution of the past from the mineral kingdom on; but evolution does not stop with so-called Homo sapiens: evolution is continuous, and our task is to carry forward and foster this great evolutionary impulse, without, however, repudiating the preceding stages!

Accepting the multiplicity of our motivations not only helps us to avoid repression but also leads to the utilization, in individually and socially productive ways, of potent energies that otherwise may erupt in harmful and destructive directions. It is analogous to the channeling of torrential waters to serve a power station. And when the tendency is excessive, it can be regulated by mobilizing another, opposite tendency against it, as occasion demands and the goal indicates: pitting ambition and the desire for possessions, for example, against laziness; or, inversely, balancing a tendency to excessive activism by cultivating a desire for the quiet life. This is one of the more subtle and effective arts of volitional action; not to oppose directly or launch frontal attacks, but to maneuver skillfully. And it is accomplished primarily through "the feeding power of attention," as was discussed in the chapters on the Skillful Will.

The third advantage of directing all psychological tendencies toward creative purposes accrues from the manner in which these tendencies, the very energies themselves, become transmuted and sublimated through being redirected to higher ends. This process of transmutation of the psychological energies has great importance and broad application. It deserves to be much better known and more widely practiced, since it constitutes the most effective and constructive method of dealing with two major and potent sources of energy—sex and aggressiveness. It has been discussed in some detail in Chapter 6 (pages 62–65).

Concerning the combining, or converging, of motives in determining decisions and the activities that result from them, we can often observe that, side by side with humanitarian reasons, other motives are present, such as ambition, vanity, the desire for recognition, the approval of others, self-assertion, etc. Therefore it is not appropriate to pass judgments of "good" and "bad," "higher" or "lower," in any absolute sense. All is *relative* to the individual, to his evolutionary stage, to his environmental circumstances, and to many other factors. To state it in an oversimplified way, what may be "good" in one is "bad" in another. The great Renaissance philosopher Tomasso Campanella observed, "In God we shall see who did and said the better thing." Thus it is the course of wisdom to follow Christ's injunction, "Judge not."

The objection might be made that every volitional act involves a *valuation*, an assessment; that is, a "value judgment." While this is true, we should not confuse two different meanings of the word "judgment" and two different ways of using it. In speaking of judgment, one usually means *moral* judgment: commendation, approval, or more often censure, condemnation, which incidentally give their user a sense of superiority. Instead, the judgments necessary in the first stage of the volitional act, and also in the second, deliberative one are (as we shall see) objective, rational evaluations, arrived at on the basis of many and diverse elements. The more precise word in this case is clear "discrimination."

In our examination of motives, then, we should recognize that the "lower" ones constitute a *subjective*, ethical imperfection, but not an *objective* obstacle; they can indeed promote the accomplishment of the more lofty activities. In the field of the arts, for example, aside from higher inspiration and spontaneous creative impulse, creativity can be stimulated and intensified by the spur of practical necessity. Two outstanding examples of this have been Balzac and Dostoevski. Both were goaded by economic need, Dostoevski because of his passion for gambling, Balzac on account of debts contracted by his luxurious style of living and his improvident habit of rewriting his novels many times when they had reached the proof stage. As it turned out, this spur caused them both to produce a greater number of works than they otherwise would have done. Yet the urge of financial stringency does not seem to have influenced the *quality* of the literary product. This is evident in the case of Balzac from the fact that one of his heaviest expenses was directly attributable to his artistic scruples, which induced him to rewrite the same work several times. The composer Rossini provides a contrasting example which constitutes a confirmation of a negative kind. When he had become rich and famous, courted and adored by "all Paris," he lacked sufficient incentive to overcome his natural laziness and epicureanism and ceased to write operas of quality. Had he been more ambitious or intent on earning more and more money, probably we would have had some more masterpieces.

Therefore the less elevated motives can not only be profitably utilized but also at times deliberately aroused: for instance, making public pledges in order to avoid the shame of not keeping them, or promising ourselves rewards of various kinds (the "carrot method"!).

Recourse to these means could be considered an act of humility, since it implies recognition of the existence in us of these lower, or simply personal, elements. What is important is to make sure that the lower motives are aligned with the higher motives, and that it is *these* that are in control and determine the action. I have specified clear-cut supremacy, but perhaps one might even be content with just a modicum of supremacy. When a group possesses fifty-one per cent of the shares of a company, it determines its policy. Analogously, in volitional action even a slight supremacy of higher motives suffices to ensure that the lower ones, even if strong, have not the say in decisions and actions, and that they remain harmless or even useful, as are the minority shareholders who bring capital.

On the other hand, it is well to be aware that all this can be accompanied by drawbacks and dangers. The will must be kept vigilant so that the lower motives may not become strengthened and prevail, leading to illusion, compromise, and deviation from the initial aim, or predetermined purpose. Moreover, all this concerns the achievement of external aims. When, instead, *inner* development, *transpersonal* realization is the goal, the (comparatively) lower drives and energies have to be transformed and sublimated through the action of the higher motives and the attractive pull of the higher goals.

Let me summarize this chapter by applying these observations to the person intent on carrying through the first stage of the act of will so that he may begin his willed act with the maximum possibility of success. That person must get his goals or purposes clearly in view. Then he must evaluate his goals. In the process of evaluation he will examine his motives, trying to become aware of the unconscious ones. It is a testing of the worthwhileness of what has been seen as a goal. My main point in this chapter has concerned the nature of motives, however. After being examined, motives must be *aroused* and *used.* Otherwise the setting of goals and the analysis of self remain only academic. Psychological energies must be set into motion and used with clear intent in the service of a higher good; must be mustered and combined so that the will can effectively proceed to action that will lead from goals to accomplishment. With this initial *zest,* a person can proceed to the deliberate examination of the ways in which he can actually achieve a given aim. Without the dynamism of his motives, no matter how clear his aims or worth while they may be, a person can lack the drive to go on and remain only a dreamer instead of the doer of willed action.

13

DELIBERATION, CHOICE, AND DECISION

There are usually a number of goals which we feel an urge to pursue. But it is not possible or practical to pursue all of them. Certainly not all at once. Therefore we must *choose* among the many possibilities the one that is most worth while, the one we *prefer*—and *decide* to pursue it, renouncing or postponing the others. This is where deliberation comes into play.

The objective of every deliberation, of every consideration of one or more possibilities, is to lead to the best possible decision. A decision reached without deliberation, without examining and evaluating all aspects of the question or choice that confronts us, can lead to impulsive, unconsidered, and ill-advised action. This may often involve us in blunders which can damage ourselves and others. The significance of the two words "unconsidered" and "ill-advised" is worth noting. The first means to be lacking in due consideration; the second, in sound counsel.

The immense number of actions that are impulsively

performed by human beings with no consideration of the consequences is appalling. This is because, in reality, few really "think." Thinking is uncomfortable and tiring; it demands concentration, and this requires a persistent use of the will. Moreover, the outcome of such thinking may unpleasantly conflict with some of our inclinations and drives. Hence, the fundamental importance, indeed the necessity, of *learning* to think properly, to reflect and to *meditate* (see Appendix Two, page 218).

The techniques for the control and the most effective utilization of one's own mind are among the most valuable in psychosynthesis. They constitute a basic preparation for deliberation—for the work of consideration and reflection that must precede a sound decision.

But to have the space needed to think, meditate, and then decide, we must keep in abeyance the tendencies and drives that impel us toward immediate action. This means taking time, the time needed to examine the situation from all angles and reflect upon it. Thus the prerequisite of thinking—and deliberation—is an act of restraint, of *inhibition.*

Inhibiting Function of the Will

Professor Calò has correctly pointed out an apparently paradoxical aspect of the will:

> The volitional act is, from one very important point of view, substantially *inhibition.* It is not, however, an automatic inhibition, like that which a tendency or the energy inherent in an idea can exercise against another tendency or idea. But it is *willed,* first against all of them, in order that deliberation itself may be possible, then in the decision against those drives which are still in competition with the chosen aim. This aspect of inhibition can be more or less striking. In some cases the entire effort of willing appears to consist only (but never does so

consist) in the effort of inhibiting certain tendencies, and to be reduced to a *non-willing;* while in other cases the decision is made so rapidly and easily that it seems to be done without the intervention of the will.

To modern ears, the word "inhibition" carries a rather unpleasant sound; it brings to mind repression and its unfortunate consequences. It can be said that today there is a veritable phobia regarding repression. Therefore, it is worth while clarifying the great difference that exists between "repression" and *conscious control.*

To repress an impulse is to condemn it, to try to obliterate it or to "bottle it up" in the unconscious and pretend that it doesn't exist. But whatever is repressed returns later, and often in disguise, to claim its due. Inhibition, on the other hand, consists in resolutely holding back an impulse or tendency while deliberating on how best to deal with it. Therefore repression is foolish. But, rightly used, inhibition can be the mark of wisdom. We may inhibit the *expression* of a stupid or harmful impulse without "repressing it." We recognize the impulse, examine and analyze it, and then direct or transmute it, or even act it out, at a more appropriate time. If we repress, we become victims of what we deny, but if we use inhibition wisely we gain freedom and mastery.

In regard to what Professor Calò says, it should be pointed out that inhibition *per se* is not a stage of the will. It is a quality that is needed not only in *preparing* for volitional action but also as a necessary condition in all stages of the will.

Deliberation

It has already been stated in the preceding chapter

that one of the chief requirements for a truly volitional act is the bringing to light and examination of unconscious motives. When this is done, we can then see to it that our conscious motives are good and that they imply acts that are constructive both for ourselves and for others. *But this is not sufficient.* It is well to be explicit on this point, because many believe that good intentions are enough.

The well-known saying "The road to hell is paved with good intentions" can be taken in two senses. The first and more obvious one refers to the inertia and weakness of so many good people. Their good intentions are not followed by decisions, affirmations, and acts, and so they remain ineffective. The other meaning refers to the bad consequences that can follow acts that are committed with the best of intentions but with little wisdom. These acts are indeed sometimes completely lacking in common sense.

Examples of this kind of mistaken action are decisions taken by some parents and imposed on their children in the sincere belief that they are "for the children's good." Such parents may push them, for instance, against their wishes, in the direction of some remunerative or prestigious career; or perhaps they protect them excessively, and thereby prevent them from gaining necessary experience on their own account (even if it involves some hardship and a reasonable amount of risk).

So the first few steps in the process of deliberation consist in *seeing clearly*, in posing the problem plainly, in formulating the alternatives with which we are faced, and in considering the path and the outcome that will follow each alternative. This approach applies to deliberating about different goals or about a single goal. In the latter case, the alternatives can pertain to different possibilities for realizing that goal, or simply to whether to pursue it or not. This clear posing of alternatives seems obvious, but very often it is not done.

Next comes the recognition, from a realistic standpoint, of the *possibility* of achieving one's purpose or purposes, and of the *appropriate time* for action. At this stage, one establishes a natural sequence for the various steps and for their timing in passing from the initial project, through the program, to the actualization of one's goal. It has been said that "politics is the art of the possible," but it could be added that a large part of wisdom, at least of practical wisdom, consists in ascertaining *what* is possible and *when* it is so. It is here that so many idealists err, nobly but with unfortunate results. They keep their eyes so fixed on the sparkling mountaintop that they do not watch where they are putting their feet—and risk stumbling and falling. Or they attempt to climb up the steep slopes of the mountain by a direct but impracticable route instead of following a winding but manageable path.

It is necessary to consider the *consequences* of the action that we are proposing to take. This is an *exercise in foresight*. It demands careful reflection and psychological discrimination, particularly when the involvement and cooperation of others are concerned. If we fail to do this, our words and acts may well produce effects very different from those we expect and desire. One of the simplest examples is to be seen when our insistence and eagerness arouse negative reactions in others. In these cases, merely mental considerations do not suffice; what is needed is *empathy*, that is, the capacity to enter, so to speak, into the skin of others, and by means of intuitive imagination, become aware of the effects our words and acts may produce.

Inspiration and Intuition

Let us now examine another way of making decisions, especially those that are determined by motives originating in or arriving via the higher unconscious (superconscious) in the form of illuminations, inspirations, and urges to action, both inner and outer. Broadly speaking, such motives can be considered transpersonal in character: artistic creativity, altruistic and humanitarian impulses, the search for truth, etc. Their origin often cannot be identified with certainty; they may be activities of the superconscious, they may come from the Higher or Transpersonal Self, or they may have other sources. But it is not necessary to ascertain where they originate. What *is* important is to *recognize* these incentives, these inspirations, to open oneself to them, and to welcome them. I have said *welcome* them because we are not always willing to do so. Sometimes they bewilder us and even arouse negative reactions, either on the part of the conscious self or from elements of the lower unconscious. In fact, these inspirations and urges often make the individual uncomfortable because they goad him to assume undertakings and take actions that call for a spirit of self-sacrifice, surrender, or risk.

On the other hand, these "inspirations" and inner urges are not to be accepted and followed without being subject to careful scrutiny. First of all, it is necessary to determine whether they are *genuine* intuitions or inspirations. In other words, do these promptings to act *really* come from the exalted level of the superconscious? We must distinguish them from those impulses that come from other levels of the unconscious or from external influences. The difference is sometimes evident, but often it is not, and its recognition can be very difficult. We live immersed in a psychic ocean, enveloped in a psychic atmosphere; we are continually subject to influences of every kind and source. Therefore a cautious attitude of continuous discrimination is necessary, particularly in the case of individuals with great psychic sensitivity.

Furthermore, even when an inspiration emanates from a truly elevated source and the intuition is genuine, serious errors can still be made in its *interpretation* and consequently in its execution. Such errors often do occur. Adequate mental development is needed to *understand* these inspirations and promptings correctly. Also, firm self-control is needed to avoid excessive emotional reactions (sometimes mounting to exaltation) and/or impulsive and fanatical behavior.

Thus, what has been said about other motives is also applicable in this case: do not let yourself be drawn *immediately* into action, but by an act of will exercise the *inhibition* that will give time for a thorough examination of the inspiration and for determining whether it is genuine and its adoption advisable.

However, although careful discrimination must be used, we should also be wary of an *excessively* critical attitude that might stifle the inspiration. Some people have a tendency to question excessively, producing doubts and confusion, although experience has shown that in many cases their original intuitive flash, the first incentive, was right. So here again balance, or in other words the use of wisdom, is needed.

These difficulties should not deter us either from using the approach of arriving at correct choices, or from following our higher promptings. On the contrary, those who do not have spontaneous inspirations or intuitions can make use of the available methods for activating the superconscious and for linking it with the conscious personality. The most reliable ones are the various procedures of *receptive* and *reflective meditation*.

These, as well as other techniques, are described in Appendix Two (see page 218). In all cases of deliberation the aim is to use well-tested practices to enlist the highest mental powers in the process of deliberation and choice. These can range from truly concentrated thinking to opening oneself to inspiration while in a state of inner silence. The reader will want to experiment with these and other meditative techniques, such as those mentioned in *Psychosynthesis*, but one which has direct application to the stage of deliberation is that of "consulting the Higher Self." Naturally, it takes some practice, and it can be gradually refined, but it consists essentially in *asking*, whether aloud, silently, or in writing, the advice of the Higher Self on a particular matter. It is surprising to find how often the answer to a difficult problem comes, sooner or later, from a source that is within us, from the highest part of us.

Consulting with Others

This is another method of arriving at decisions, one that is, incidentally, useful for checking on the validity of any inner promptings. It can be of great help, but, like any other single technique, it is often the source of drawbacks and errors. Its success depends as much on the attitude adopted and the method used by the seeker of advice as on those of the giver. However, many situations can greatly benefit from its use, particularly when the decisions involve others. It is most advisable, of course, when we are not certain of our ability to judge correctly, either for want of information or because we lack competence in the particular subject matter.

The many advantages of this method are not always

recognized. In the first place, the very process of telling our problem to another person helps us to *formulate it clearly*, to "objectify" it, so to speak, and thus to understand it better. Sometimes, simply the act of stating a problem in clear terms brings out the solution and lets us see the way to go, even before the other person responds. Apart from this, the questions of the person we are consulting, *his* way of considering the matter, often put it in a different light and make us aware of other possible points of view. Moreover, our verbal expression can serve to discharge the emotions aroused by the situation and thus to reduce or eliminate this great source of confusion and mistakes. The act of precise formulation also helps us to curb the often restless overactivity of the mind and compels it to think in an orderly way.

Finally, there is also the subtle and indefinable but genuine effect of the mere *presence* of a willing and understanding listener. This can be said to be "catalytic" because it is analogous to the role performed in a chemical reaction by a substance that does not itself form part of a compound but whose presence makes possible or accelerates the reaction. This chemical action has not yet been fully explained but it is very effective. Here again, just as we do not have to understand the exact nature of catalysis in order to make use of it, we can take advantage of the very substantial effect of a sympathetic listener to help us make decisions without being able clearly to define the process.

The difficulties in consulting others arise when the motive of the enquirer is to evade his own responsibilities and indulge in the tendency present in many people to lean on others, to give them indiscriminate credence, and to be blinded or at least strongly influenced by their prestige or by their presumed authority. Much recent worship of therapists, political leaders, gurus, and others stems from this tendency to escape from responsibility and freedom. This can be considered as a manifestation of the general tendency to rely on external authorities, something which has happened over and over again against the will of genuine teachers and sages. One thinks of the Roman followers of Pythagoras who used, as a final answer: *Ipse dixit* ("*He* said it!"). Another instance is that of the authority accorded to Aristotle, which had a hampering influence on thought throughout the Middle Ages and aroused, in the Renaissance, bitter attacks against those who dared to question it.

Another disadvantage can occur when we turn to a number of people for advice; their frequently contrasting opinions may increase our uncertainty. In addition, a person seeking advice lays himself open to a further pitfall. He may indeed be the recipient of well-defined and pertinent advice, but this deprives him of the opportunity of arriving at a decision by himself, gaining useful experience, and thereby developing this aspect of the will. Excessive interference on the part of those whose advice has not been asked may account for the reaction expressed in the well-known reply, "Don't tell me what to do; I can make my own mistakes!"

Counseling

Nevertheless, there is a *correct counseling technique* which is worth learning. A careful choice of the terms to be used is of value in determining the attitude to be taken and the mode of procedure to be adopted by both parties. Instead of talking in terms of "asking advice," it is better to say "consulting." The person to whom we address ourselves, instead of pontificating as an "adviser," assumes the role of a "consultant" who provides information and an opinion. There are several ways in which a consultant can help:

1. By assisting one to formulate clearly the problem to be deliberated upon—the question to be solved—by assembling and working out all the relevant and useful data and information, and then by coordinating them in such a way as to pose the matter in its clearest possible terms.

2. When the problem concerns relations with other individuals (for instance, one's children, spouse, parents, employer, or subordinates), by helping one to see that due consideration is given to *their* points of view. Even intelligent and sensitive people may suffer from specific blind spots that allow them to make unfair and excessive demands on others. They are honestly surprised when their expectations provoke hostile and even violent reactions.

3. By directing attention to the inevitable *consequences* of the various possible choices and by illustrating how certainly the *law of cause and effect* is likely to respond to one's actions. A consultant can present not only the consequences of a particular outer action but also the equally real consequences of a particular inner, psychological, action. We easily forget that psychological decisions have definite psychological effects.

4. By assisting the enquirer in finding the correct interpretations of the impressions and indications that he has received from unconscious and especially superconscious urges and intuitions.

The method of consultation can be employed very simply, in the form of *dialogue*. The dialogue method is not new; the most famous exemplar of it was Socrates, as recorded by Plato. One is struck by Socrates's skillful and shrewd procedure, and by the subtle art with which he leads his interlocutor to the personal discovery of the truth and to the adoption of a clear way of thinking. The method of the dialogue has recently been accorded renewed validation, particularly by Martin Buber and Ira Progoff, and is finding increasing application in psychotherapy. Various forms of dialogue have been given serious consideration by Paul Tournier and his associates in the movement called "Medicine of the Personality." A meeting of this group in Zurich in 1967 was devoted to various aspects of the dialogue: the dialogue for the general practitioner; the marital dialogue; parapsychology and dialogue; the dialogue for the psychiatrist; the dialogue with God; the dialogue in meditation.

Meditating with others is also very helpful and the experienced individual can teach its technique and direct a group effectively. Moreover, to stay silent together promotes a catalytic action and facilitates the "descent" of intuitions and inspirations.

Collective Deliberation

This method of deliberating has always been in use (for good or ill). The modern world is employing it increasingly, assisted by the rapidity of communication. It has its specific advantages, but is not devoid of shortcomings. Its most obvious advantage is the opportunity that it provides for revealing and defining the different facets of the problem situation that is to be resolved, by allowing it to be considered from the various points of view contributed by the diverse skills of each member of the group. Because this procedure pools and balances each one's qualities, there is an enhanced probability that unanimous or majority decisions thus arrived at will turn out to be both fair and appropriate.

This is the democratic method in the best sense of the word; but good results depend on whether all who share in the deliberation adopt an objective and dispassionate approach and are animated by a sincere intention to arrive at the best possible solution. It would be naïve to expect this to happen always. In many cases, preconceptions, individual and group prejudices, and, not least, the obstinacy and pique aroused by pride will induce some participants to attempt to impose their personal opinions without truly listening to the ideas of others.

Moreover, not infrequently the pros and cons which have emerged from the various aspects of the discussion seem to balance each other out and to block a clear-cut decision. This begets uncertainties and leads to the decision to postpone the decision.

Examples of this are plentiful, and the greater the number of consultants, the more likely it is to happen. As the humorist P. Lafitte remarked, "One administrator administers; three administrators study the best way of administering; five administrators discuss conflicting programs; seven administrators chatter."

And yet, in spite of the serious defects of this consultative method, the dictatorial, or authoritarian, system with its power of decision residing in the hands of a single individual is more perilous and opens the door to real disaster. Camille Cavour, the Italian Prime Minister of the kingdom of Piedmont, had this to say: "I prefer the worst Chamber of Deputies to the best royal Antechamber." Moreover, in many cases collective deliberation and decision are unavoidable.

Let us see, then, how it can be regulated, so as both to limit its defects and to utilize what advantages it offers. The first rule is to *reduce to a minimum* the number of those who are to have a hand in the decisions. This does not exclude the participation of experts in the examination of the question, but it limits them to a consultative role. Another rule is to put time limits on both discussion and decision. A third, and important, rule demands that those who make the decisions *assume all responsibility for them*, as a group no less than as individuals.

In addition to these general rules for the method of collective deliberation, there are others to be applied according to the different situations that call for decision. I cannot deal with them here except to advocate that the decisions each of us finds himself having to make with others be conducted as much as possible on a *basis of equality*. The proper attitude to take can be summed up in this simple, practical formula: "Let us not argue, but look for the best solution together." This demands of each the preparation already recommended for individual deliberation, that is to say, the examination of personality motives and reasons.

Individual Differences

At this point, it seems appropriate to discuss the factor of "characterological differences." So far, the subject of deliberation and decision has been dealt with in a general way. But here, too, as in every psychological issue, there are often marked *personal differences* that should be taken into full account. Methods should be adapted to each psychological type. Applying this to the subject under examination, we must first of all distinguish two opposite human types: the "impulsive" and the "indecisive." What I have said so far applies in particular to the impulsives. Impulsive people need to practice, often, all the techniques of calm deliberation, inhibition, and meditation.

The indecisives, who represent a minority, call for a

different approach. They must be faced with the *necessity* for making decisions. They must learn to do so by seizing opportunities "on the fly," at the right moment. There is an Oriental maxim that has significance for both types: "One cannot mount a camel that has not yet arrived, or one that has already departed."

We can distinguish two different causes, or groups of causes, of indecision. One, which may be considered "constitutional," occurs in introverted types who indulge in excessive and sterile self-analysis. They often have an intense sense of inferiority. Here, an important distinction should be made between a *feeling* of inferiority or superiority and an inferiority or superiority *complex*. This word "complex" is used in a rather loose fashion, whereas it should be reserved for serious, even pathological, cases. Everyone has a *sense* of superiority or inferiority. This represents no "complex" but is simply an inner attitude that is usually well within the bounds of normality. We are all superior in some things and inferior in others. But the introvert's general feeling of inferiority, or even his inferiority complex, is usually not justified, because he is frequently intelligent and gifted with aesthetic and moral sensitivity.

Other causes of indecision are *conflicts* between unconscious and conscious motives, *fear* of making a mistake, and *unwillingness* to assume responsibility. (This last is sometimes due to regrets for mistakes committed in the past.) Psychotherapeutic assistance or self-psychotherapy can help to reveal these causes and to eliminate them.

Indecisives must clearly recognize that *to decide is inevitable*. As has already been mentioned, not to decide is in itself a decision, and may well be the worst one! They have to develop *the courage to make mistakes*. They must recognize that errors are rarely irremediable, and often prove productive as sources of experience. Science and technology continually employ the trial-and-error method. Indecisives are sometimes reduced to a state of dithering uncertainty by small choices of no importance. At such times, a *toss-up* decision is in order.

Two other psychological types should be kept distinct from those just mentioned. They are the *obstinate* and the *changeable*. An indecisive, once he has laboriously arrived at a decision, may cling to it tenaciously, while an impulsive can be easily swayed, uncritically and without self-control, by alternating impulses to act. On the other hand, obstinacy can be the effect of pride, or of a mental rigidity which restricts the field of view to only *one* aspect of a many-sided and changing reality. These people can be helped to see clearly the difference between obstinacy and will, which can be confused at a superficial level of observation. Many believe and maintain they have a strong will when they are merely stubborn!

As for changeableness, it can originate in a too open and plastic mind which sees some validity in every alternative and recognizes the continual renewal of life in constantly changing forms. Changeable people need to realize that there *are* unchanging laws governing the evolution of life, and that our decisions can be taken and upheld in harmony with them.

All psychological types can undertake the adjustment of their character excesses and limitations by bringing the *will* into play in different and sometimes opposite ways, but always with clear vision, decision, and wisdom. The acts of deliberation and decision require mental alertness, adequate preparation, vigilance, and self-control; in short, a resolute and continual application of the *will*.

Choice

A fundamental fact of which we should be clearly aware is that to "decide" very often means to *choose*; that is, a selection must be made from among various possibilities. But to choose implies to *prefer*; and to prefer some one thing, one action, one way, necessarily demands the discarding or eliminating of others, i.e., their *relinquishment*. This is obvious, or should be, and thus easily accepted. Yet in practice it arouses strong resistance and reluctance, often indeed violent rebellion. The very words "renunciation" and "sacrifice" * excite intense aversion. Various causes are at the root of these reactions:

1. Hedonism, i.e., the fundamental desire for pleasure and for the avoidance of suffering, which is innate in human nature.

2. The exaggerated emphasis placed in the past on duty and sacrifice, and the excessive insistence on the value of suffering, often for wrong or needless reasons.

3. An erroneous conception of liberty, which has been interpreted as the right to follow every impulse and satisfy every desire without concern for the consequences to ourselves or to others, with complete lack of restraint or sense of responsibility.

From all this springs a more or less conscious "refusal to choose" when a choice is clearly needed. It represents an attempt to "have one's cake and eat it too." (And thus leads to frustration, double binds, inner conflict, loss of opportunity, and exactly that unnecessary suffering which it was the original desire to avoid!)

As was previously pointed out, an important criterion in choosing is to foresee in the clearest possible manner what *effects* the choice will have: not only the immediate but also the long-term ones, since the latter can turn out

* It is interesting and illuminating to realize that rather than meaning a painful self-inflicted asceticism, the word "sacrifice" means "to make holy," "to make sacred" (*sacrum facere*).

to be different from, and indeed opposite to, the former. Something that is immediately satisfactory can have harmful effects later.

The ability to select from alternatives and the wisdom to choose well can, like all other functions, be developed by means of methodical training incorporating appropriate exercises. This training can best be begun with the making of decisions and choices about matters of little or no importance in themselves. By eliminating, for the moment, every element of personal interest or selfish gratification, the pure inner act by which a decision is made can be isolated. It may be exercised through the choice of taking one street in preference to another, or, similarly, when in a restaurant by choosing one dish instead of the others. Everyone can make up numerous exercises of the sort.

These can then be followed by choices between alternatives of growing importance, keeping always in mind that a choice is a *preference* which therefore implies the elimination and giving up of alternatives. It is also important to realize that, if one wants to accomplish an *aim* to which a value is attributed, one must also will the *means* of pursuing it, however unpleasant and painful they may be. A simple and effective help in achieving this is to call often to mind and repeat the affirmation, "It *is* worth the effort." Thus, the choice and its associated renunciations can be made with good grace, even cheerfully.

In the matter of making choices, it is essential to recognize that there usually are a few basic choices that enter into the many specific choices. A specific fundamental one is *the choice between the past and the future*. We are in a period of drastic change and rapid renewal; many old forms do not work any more. The old ways of life prove increasingly inadequate to meet present needs. Therefore it is vain to remain attached to them and to delude ourselves by thinking that we can preserve them intact. On the other hand, the new is not to be chosen in a hurry and without discernment. At present we are witnessing violent, excessive, and ill-considered attempts to change everything at once. The renewal can and should be regulated by appropriate choices, wise decisions, and a firm will. We should not abandon established ways without having found new and better ones. But once we have found new ways, we must have the courage and the will to throw ourselves boldly and joyfully into the adventure which the future holds.

14

AFFIRMATION

From what has been said thus far it would appear that the act of will is a complex and time-consuming process. It is, but only if we mean the complete and self-conscious act. Certainly, when a person is contemplating important changes in his life he should endeavor to work through all the six stages. But such occasions are rare and one need not delve into motives, engage consultants, or work out elaborate charts of causes and probable effects in order to crack the morning egg. Still, it is important to realize that many of us fail in numerous actions of intermediate importance because of difficulties in some specific stage of the will. Perhaps we do not examine motives; or we are indecisive; or we have not learned to deliberate thoroughly. From a study and understanding of the six stages we can learn *how* to use our will, *where* we typically fail, and *what* exercises to use to overcome our deficiencies. We can then move to correct deficiencies in the general pattern, and this will automatically improve each small daily act of will. And we will live more freely, more in harmony with life and our own true purposes.

Affirmation is a pivotal stage in the act of willing. Once the stages of *deliberation, choice,* and *decision* have been carried through, there comes the phase of *achievement,* so that what is willed *shall be, happen,* or *manifest itself.* The first step or act of this phase consists in *affirmation.* Without it, the decision remains latent, lacking a dynamic impelling power. Affirmation is therefore an essential "moment," or stage, of the will. This is the meaning of Spinoza's observation, "The Will is the power of affirming or denying." The word "power" should be well noted; it means two things: power in the sense of capacity, and power as potency, or energy.

Let us realize what is implied and required by volitional affirmation, or the *affirmative will.* Fundamentally, it is a sense, or state of mind, of *certainty.* This has two aspects, or better, is the synthesis of two inner attitudes: *faith* and *conviction.* True faith is by nature intuitive; it perceives the reality of what is not evident, not manifested, and accepts it. According to Saint Paul's definition, it is the "substance of things hoped for, the evidence of things not seen." Faith leading to a sense of certainty requires primarily *faith in oneself,* that is, in the real Self, in what we are essentially. Keyserling says it very effectively: "Only that inward affirmation which is called faith creates the decision which 'makes real' the Self in phenomenal existence. . . . This living spirit," says Keyserling, "the metaphysical kernel of man's being, is neither understanding nor reason, nor any particular function whatsoever: it is substance. . . . It is in the true sense of the word what is most substantive in man. That is why it has qualities, but is not one in itself."

Conviction is by nature mental; it is reached either by way of reason or through intellectual adherence to an intuition recognized as being in harmony with truth. In living experience, faith and conviction coexist and are blended in varying proportion. Their combination results in *certainty.*

To be effective, affirmation must be vigorous; it must possess a strong dynamic potential, or intensity. To employ an analogy taken from electricity, this might be called a high psychological "voltage." Affirmation may be considered a *command,* a command given with *authority.* Authority may proceed from a position of responsibility or some function in the external world, but it is especially and essentially an inner quality, an inner reality, psychological or spiritual. Whoever exercises it feels, indeed *knows,* that he possesses it, and those to whom it is directed perceive it directly. This authority can, and indeed should, be exercised particularly on the psychological energies and functions within us that we need to use to achieve our purpose.

The Techniques of Affirmation

Affirmation is made effective through the use of precise techniques.

1. *The use of "words of power."* A verbal affirmation, to be effective, must be expressed in a clear, exact way. Sometimes a single word suffices, but often it is better expressed through a short phrase or formula. The words or phrases can be said only inwardly, but are more effective if pronounced aloud—that is, with the added power of sound—or, if put in writing or printed, observed intently. Men have collectively acknowledged the power of words and phrases by remembering them, even when the context that produced them has been forgotten. It is just this seemingly magic power which one can mobilize in using this technique. The words or phrases to be used

naturally differ and must be chosen in accordance with the objective we are aiming at, with what we want to evoke and develop in ourselves. A list of some having general application is given at the end of the chapter.

2. *The use of images.* Images constitute another means through which affirmations can be focused; their dynamic potency is well known. One can use the image, or vision, of what is wanted *as if it were already accomplished* (the "ideal model" of the personality and the technique of "acting as if" used in psychosynthesis are examples of this). Or one can use an image that is the *symbol* of what we will to realize. To affirm his decision to make the will skillful, for example, one might visualize an orchestra and its conductor. In this case, one must also keep in mind the original purpose of which the image is a symbol. Images can either be visualized mentally, or some external image, a drawing, a picture, etc., can be selected and observed closely. Placing such images near where we work, for example, can keep an affirmation alive and vivid during all our working hours.

3. *Assuming physical attitudes.* That is, making gestures, performing acts, which either directly or symbolically express what is to be achieved. The ancient use of mudra is an example of the affirmative use of gesture.

4. *Repetition.* This also is an important and indeed often needed technique. What one wills to accomplish may need to be reaffirmed as a command a great many times. The same applies to the use of images and external acts. The required number of repetitions depends on the importance of the aim, the difficulty of its attainment, and the time needed for the process of manifestation. When this is protracted, the repetitions must be the expression of a persistent, inner affirmative attitude.

The technique of repetition can be employed in a variety of ways:

a. Repetition *at definite times* of the same words or phrases, or repeated use of the same images; for instance, at certain moments of the day (on waking, before going to sleep, etc.).

b. Series of repetitions at more or less long intervals.

c. Repetition with *variations of form*. This method avoids the drawback of the repetitions becoming routine and mechanical. Variations revive interest and stimulate imagination.

Different criteria according to the specific situation and aim must determine the choice among these various ways, but it is chiefly through experimenting that we can ascertain which way or combination of ways is most effective. Much can be learned about repetition from three groups of people who differ greatly from one another: composers, dictators, and advertisers. Composers will make repeated use of a musical motive or variations of it in the course of a sonata or symphony. This has been adopted to create a specific musical form, of which Beethoven's thirty-two variations on a theme is an outstanding example. An instance of insistent, unvaried repetition of a theme is Ravel's "Bolero."

Dictators employ the technique of repetition to an extreme degree. It is the process of "hammering home" an idea, and what is called today brain-washing. They do it consciously; Hitler candidly stated in *Mein Kampf* that he did it. I think it was he who said that one can make people believe any falsehood if only it is repeated often enough! This is the method deliberately used in systematic propaganda.

Advertisers are probably the cleverest in the use of repetition and, in general, in influencing people by means of affirmation. They use the same advertisement for a considerable time and then modify it or change it altogether. Recently a big oil firm asked the public if they should continue to use a certain slogan associated with an image or change it. Having aroused renewed interest in this way, they continued to use it. Their formulas and images are chosen, often on expert psychological advice, in order to appeal to basic human motivations. Study of their methods can suggest more valuable ways of employing them for higher purposes than the merchandising of chewing gum.

The use of affirmations demands special caution. One should make sure, at this stage, to have checked that his predominant motive is right, good, and harmless. Another point to be careful about in making affirmations is to avoid so far as possible arousing contrary reactions on the part of others. Affirmations can be more effective if made in a calm, quiet, nonaggressive manner. In this connection, however, a reservation is in order; the reaction of the conscious mind and that of the unconscious can frequently be different and even opposite. We sometimes react negatively to certain repeated, insistent repetitions, but this does not prevent our unconscious from being "impressed" and inducing us to act in accordance with the suggestion or affirmation. Television publicity is an example of this. At the conscious level, it can arouse reactions of boredom and antagonism, but then one often finds oneself buying the product so insistently advertised. It happens through mental laziness while shopping, or as an automatic reaction while thinking about something else. This provides confirmation of the coexistence in us of different tendencies, even subpersonalities, sometimes opposed to each other.

In the use of the technique of affirmation, all hurry and impatience to see results are to be avoided. Affirmations often not only do not give immediate and evident results, they can produce at first contrary effects by bringing to light hidden opposing forces. This is no reason for discouragement; it may indeed perform a useful function. It is well that such opposition reveals itself, for this makes us aware of its existence and permits us to confront it openly and master it. As is well known, the principal technique of psychoanalysis is to bring to light the "resistances" of the patient and eliminate them.

An important point in using inner affirmations, that is, in addressing commands to the various psychological functions (thought, imagination, etc.) is to do so from a certain "inner distance," from "above," so to speak, without identifying oneself with them. Instead, given the close relationship between the "I," the center of self-awareness and the will (as indicated in the diagram of the psychological functions, page 13), one can well identify himself with his will. Before and besides using various affirmations for the different volitional actions, it is most effective to use what could be called the basic, the essential affirmation:

I AM A WILL; I AM A CONSCIOUS, POTENT, DYNAMIC *WILL*

Also the close connection between the will, the self, and love can be emphasized through affirming:

I AM A LIVING, LOVING, WILLING SELF

It should be apparent that much of what is said in this book faces two ways at once: one toward the use of the will to accomplish a variety of purposes, the other toward using the will to train the will itself, as a prior or concurrent activity. Happily there tends to be a constant interaction—every act of the will trains the will and each bit of training allows for further acts of will. If we keep this fact in mind, the will will be present in our consciousness as we act. This is in itself a good technique for developing the will.

Words and Phrases of Power

There is an unlimited variety of words and phrases from which each reader can choose those he feels are suited to his needs. A list of "evocative words," which can be used quite effectively as "words of power," can be found on page 78. Here I shall suggest a few phrases, taken from the inscriptions on the coats of arms of various noble families:

Ad sidera vultus—Face toward the stars
Pensa al fine—Think of the goal
Bien faire et laisser dire—Act well and let people talk
Semper vigilans—Ever watchful
In tutto armonia—In everything, harmony

15

PLANNING AND
PROGRAMING

If we observe contemporary life, a curious contradiction presents itself. Planning and programing are often talked about today, and much economic, social, and technical planning is being done. On the other hand, separate individuals often live with no well-defined personal plan and without having a clear and conscious life program.

Yet a fundamental condition for successful planning of all kinds is the *planning and programing of the personal life*—primarily in a psychological sense, i.e., in the sense of carrying out one's individual psychosynthesis and the various interpersonal and social psychosyntheses. This personal planning must be done in accordance with the general rules and techniques appropriate to planning of any other kind. Therefore let us briefly examine these rules and techniques.

The most important rule is to *formulate,* clearly and precisely, *the goal to be reached,* and then to *retain it unswervingly in mind* throughout all the stages of the execution, which are often long and complex. This is no easy thing! Indeed, one may say that it presents great difficulty, since in man there is a constant tendency to pay excessive attention to the means he must employ to gain his end, even to the point of making him lose sight of it. The means ever tend to become ends in themselves, and when this happens, *man becomes enslaved by the means he has chosen to employ.*

Nowhere can this be seen more clearly than in the current much debated problem of the interaction between man and machine. In its essential terms, this problem, or better, this relationship, can be formulated thus: man creates and constructs machines in order that they may increase his power and capacity in the actions designed to achieve his ends. Thus the intended function and value of the machine are purely *instrumental* and relative to the purpose for which it has been constructed. But man very often lets himself be bewitched by his machines, overvaluing them; and instead of possessing them, he ends by being possessed by them.

The car affords striking evidence of this. The true and proper function of the car is to provide a faster and more comfortable means of arriving at a place we desire to go for a given purpose. Yet little by little man has unwittingly made of the car an object of prestige, a status symbol, a means of self-assertion, an outlet for the repressed tendencies of his life. The results have reached the grotesque. Rather than using the power of our technology to increase the safety of the car and reduce its pollution, we have needlessly increased its bulk, power, and therefore fuel consumption. This has given no real benefit, but on the contrary has helped to create such a general traffic and parking congestion, and to make of the car such an environmental menace, that its original value as a fast and comfortable means of transportation is rapidly reaching the vanishing point. Clearly our technology is not at fault, as some people tend to feel. The fault is rather in the *uses* we made of that technology when we failed to keep in mind the original goal or purpose.

The phenomenon is similar to what occurs in connection with that other "means," *money,* which also tends easily to become an end in itself through the attachment it arouses. And so we find the tendency to amass money without employing it usefully, as misers have done in all ages. Therefore, I repeat, a vigilant and energetic will is indispensable for maintaining the means "in their place," for always being master of them, *while using only those that truly serve the intended purpose, and to the extent that they serve it.* This is a fundamental rule of a right program.

Another basic consideration concerns the *possibility of a given program being realized*—in other words, its feasibility. A frequent error is to conceive plans and programs whose magnitude would demand capacities, circumstances, and resources we are very far from having at our disposal. The making of grandiose plans is something pleasant, even fascinating, and this I think we all experience. The world teems with idealists and dreamers who conceive or, more accurately, are dominated by, beautiful but impractical programs. If one comes to realize that his program is too ambitious, he should be willing to acknowledge the fact, *even if he has already started on the program.* To do otherwise would end only in frustration and other ill effects. Our organism rebels at the impossible, and many people have been victims of the compulsive Victorian will. One must be prepared after adequate consideration and testing to adjust his aspirations and programs rationally and cheerfully to realistic possibilities.

This brings us to *another rule in planning*: the establishment whenever possible of *right cooperation*. A frequent reason for the failure of so many plans lies in the fact that people want to carry out their programs themselves; *they themselves* want to be at the center of the planned organization. Thus they are often guilty of duplication through trying to do what others are already doing, sometimes with much greater resources and possibilities. What are needed are the wisdom and humility to acknowledge what has already been done, or is in preparation, in the same direction as our projects, and then to cooperate, or perhaps associate ourselves with those who are doing or propose to do the same thing.

In this context, I may recall an occurrence that has various psychologically interesting aspects. The second half of the nineteenth century saw the beginning of the construction of railway sleeping cars in America. There were two rival firms in the field, Carnegie and Westinghouse. The competition between them caused Carnegie to recognize that it would be far more profitable to combine with rather than fight his competitor. At first Westinghouse was somewhat stiff and suspicious when Carnegie asked him to meet him and discuss the matter; but little by little he warmed to the idea of amalgamating the two firms. All of a sudden, however, he stopped and asked, "But what is the new firm to be called?" "Westinghouse, naturally"; whereupon Westinghouse said, "Done!" Little comment is needed, I think. Carnegie made light of any question of *amour propre* or name in consideration of the outcome's usefulness and common interest. The other's ambition was gratified, and so they came to an agreement. If the rule of cooperation can be successfully used by businessmen for material aims, we should be willing to use it for other aims, especially higher ones!

The possibility of cooperation and its benefits are frequently ignored by those having high motives: those with a zeal to serve the world are too often also possessed by the desire to *see themselves* serving the world. Thus one frequently observes needless competition over secondary matters among schools of thought in education, psychology, and many other useful fields. A greater willingness for cooperative service and practical synthesis, implemented by concentrating on the similarities, and not on the differences, would be much more productive.

A fourth rule of planning pertains to *recognizing, distinguishing,* and *giving proper sequence* to the various phases of planning. They are *formulation; programing; structuring; project-making; model,* or *pilot, project.*

A good illustration of these stages is the case of a student of mine who wanted to develop his ability to operate from motives other than materialistic ones (safety, security, eminence, riches), which were driving him, in a compulsive way, into depression. His aim was to embrace higher values in his actions, but he feared that in so doing he would lose material comforts. After deliberating, we decided to plan a strategy to get him in touch with his higher values and gradually allow him to embrace them. This general *formulation* was the first stage of planning. The next stage was *programing.* The program called for beginning slowly, in a nonthreatening manner, by *gradually* reducing the time spent on material things. This was done in a number of steps: first, the student was asked to become *fully* aware of how his materialistic drives influenced him. Then he was asked to choose which ones he would like to reduce. Effective planning required this gradual approach, and good *structuring* dictated that awareness be followed by choice, rather than having choice early in the process. The *project* called for, among other things, ways of expanding awareness of the materialistic drives. We settled on an *experimental pilot project* which consisted of an evening review, to be made by the student before retiring, of the sway that materialistic thoughts, feelings, or actions had had upon him during the day. Once he recognized the extent of their harmful influence, this awareness became a more than sufficient *motive* to implement the *intention* to reduce them.

Thus he gradually was able to create some space in his life, and we were ready to deal with the main goal he had always had in mind—that of getting in touch with the part of himself that truly did hold higher values. The project was then expanded to include ways he could use to bring these values more and more actively into his life. It was at this point that he had the realization that acting from this higher place within him in no way meant that he had to renounce all material comforts.

Thus we can see that *formulation* stands for the initial stage in a general sense, for the conception of the plan in its broad lines. *Programing* represents a greater precision and more concrete development of the plan, particularly in the early phases of its execution. The difference may be said to correspond to that between strategic and tactical plans. Having formulated a well-defined and *structured* program, one can pass on to the working out of a definite *project* with all the practical data that relate to it. An adequately developed project can then be followed by an experimental *pilot project*. Its central aim is to *test* the project, and as such it can be very instructive, since practical experience often gives different results from those expected.

While these stages imply a gradual step-by-step process, they must all be kept in mind together. Mountain-climbing is a good example of this. The peak to be climbed has first to be selected, then the best route to the summit, which may have to be circuitous to avoid obstacles; and last, once the climb begins, the choice of footholds, which can determine the difference between safety and falling.

It may be said that a "trifocal vision" is required; that is, the perception and retention in mind of the distant goal and purpose; the survey of the intermediate stages which extend from the point of departure to the arrival; and the awareness of the next step to be taken.

This view of the whole, graduated at the same time in its different stages, can be applied to every kind of task and considered a "spatial" conception in both an objective and a symbolic sense. But as important, if not more so, is the "temporal" factor, that is, the consideration of the *timing* and *duration* each stage should have. As we know, time and space are intimately related as two aspects of the same continuum. Therefore it is a matter of implementing each stage at the right time and for the necessary period. Every phase has its most favorable, even its only possible, moment for execution, which may be expressed in the paradoxical phrase "The impossible of today is tomorrow's possible; today's possible is the impossible of tomorrow."

Another requirement to be considered is the *flexibility* of the plan, that is, its susceptibility to modification as new developments occur. Life is full of the unexpected, and however prescient one tries to be, something unforeseen very often crops up. So we must be ready to modify and *adapt* our plans. Flexibility can be seen in its simplest and most accessible form in chess, in which a player plans a series of moves to checkmate his opponent but must be on the alert to change his plan in response to the offensive moves of his opponent, who also has a similar plan.

To achieve all this demands reflection, a fine sense of proportion, and good judgment, all of which can be summed up in one simple word: *wisdom*. But unflagging attention, vigilance, patience, and persistence, which are qualities of the *will*, are also needed; which shows that planning plays an integrating part in the process of *willing*, in effective *volition*.

All these rules can and should be applied in psychosynthesis. Individual psychosynthesis can be said to consist essentially in the actualization of one's own *ideal model*. The role of planning in both the discovery and the actualization of the ideal model is fully discussed in *Psychosynthesis* (pages 166–77). Careful planning and patient execution of a life plan and subplans are necessary if one is to fulfill his personal existence and become all that he can. Needless to say, planning also belongs in the transpersonal or spiritual phase of psychosynthesis. In carrying out a psychosynthetic program, we should apply the general rules of planning, but we should also be careful to include in the process the phases of elaboration and gestation, allowing them the time they need, without interference.

Moreover, the individual life plan must be coordinated, integrated, and harmonized with plans that include other people. Individual psychosynthesis is not, and cannot be, an end in itself, since each one of us is closely linked in life with other persons and groups. We can begin this process by formulating and carrying out plans and programs enabling us to play our various *roles* in human relations and to fulfill the various functions they demand. The life of a family regarded as a psychological entity, for example, can be consciously planned and organized. Naturally, affection and good will constitute its basis, but these *are not sufficient.*

Then there are the roles associated with work, which frequently involve relations with superiors, colleagues, and subordinates. There are the community roles arising out of membership in social groups, and participation in their specific activities, political, economic, cultural, and humanitarian.

Some of the techniques of individual psychosynthesis can be usefully applied in planning and carrying out interpersonal and group psychosynthesis. Among those of more general use, I may mention the techniques for the transformation of energies, the techniques of the methodical use of images, and that of imaginative training. Conversely, interpersonal and group relations and external activities can be utilized as occasions and instruments for inner development and actualization.

A Note on Social Psychosynthesis

Social psychosynthesis raises the problem, much discussed at the present time, of the relations between the individual and society. Most of the writers who have dealt with this subject have done so in a controversial way, contrasting the two and regarding them as almost necessarily in conflict. Yet in this case, as in many other instances, it is more often a matter of dealing with a *polarity.* The principles expounded in my pamphlet *Balancing and Synthesis of Opposites* (New York, 1972) can find here a useful application. There I have used a diagram to show the relationship between each pair of opposite poles and the ways of their balancing. In reference to the problem of the individual versus society, we have the following triangular relationships:

Transformation

Conformity — Adaptation — Rebellion

At the extremities of the base of the triangle are the two opposite poles, *conformity* and *rebellion*; the middle point of the base may be taken to represent a position of compromise, allowing to a degree of maneuvering, but limiting and unsatisfactory as a lasting solution. Yet there exists a point *above*, equidistant from both poles and *at a higher level*, from which one can be an integral and effective member of society while maintaining his independence fully. This position stands *for action in and on society, in order to transform it.*

The synthetic formula for resolving this problem has been given in the Bible: "Render unto Caesar the things that are Caesar's, and unto God the things that are God's." A way of expressing this in modern psychological terms might be, "Concede to society what is necessary and appropriate, and also act in society as a constructive force for improving it." This can be done by first reserving one's own integrity and independence, "cultivating the inner garden." It is thus not a question of passively submitting to social conditioning, but first of protecting oneself from it, without resorting either to violent rebellion or to withdrawal, and then actively seeking to modify and improve present social life in every possible way.

It is important not only for society's good but also for the individual's satisfaction that he experience this inner independence. The liberty to which the individual really aspires, more or less consciously, is chiefly a *psychological* and *spiritual* freedom; but its achievement depends in large measure *on himself.* Groups and society can obstruct it in a variety of ways with their pressures, but cannot really prevent it. One can be inwardly free even while assenting to the performance of his functions and to playing his parts in the family and society, in accordance with the situation in which he finds himself. Here also the techniques of psychosynthesis can be of great assistance, especially those of "identification" and "acting as if." Using such techniques one can always have "inner space," that is, making room in consciousness, and "temporal space," or some free time, in which an independent individual life can be lived. And this does not demand long periods of time and special conditions. It is a matter of utilizing the "dimension of intensity": a half hour lived at a high level intensely can give value, meaning, and justification to a whole day.

Finally, there is a higher and broader kind of planning, which is in reality the most important; it is that of integrating the individual plan in the Universal Plan, to which I referred earlier. While we are unable to be aware of the complete scope of that Plan in its great mystery, we can at least know something of it and glimpse its broad lines and especially its evolutionary direction, and thus recognize it is the direction of the greatest *good.* This is what counts! Our first goal is not to discern the point of arrival, but to place ourselves in the right current, on the right road. Here also, and above all here, *wisdom* is necessary for harmoniously interweaving the individual plan in the Universal Plan; and will is needed for retaining a firm control of the rudder and proceeding on a straight course.

16

THE DIRECTION OF
THE EXECUTION

An examination of this final stage of volitional action will reveal the fundamental error generally committed in the use of the will, an error based upon a mistaken conception of its nature and way of functioning. This error consists in attempting to act by *imposing* the power of the will on the organs of action. Instead, the true and natural function of the will at this stage is to *direct* the execution, to put into operation the necessary and appropriate means for reaching the proposed objective. It does so by taking command of and directing the various psychophysical functions.

This will appear more clearly if we examine in detail the analogy between the activity of willing and that of driving a car. The *direct* effort of will resembles that made by a driver trying to propel his car forward by pushing it from behind with muscle power. Such behavior is manifestly absurd; and yet equally misguided is the effort to use the will for *direct* action rather than for action through the other psychological functions.

Let us examine what the driver of a car actually does. He begins by doing what corresponds to the previously described stages. He first *chooses* where he wishes to go; then he *decides* to go there and when to start. This leads to a study of the route and the *planning* of the journey.

Now comes the stage of the *direction of the execution*. It is divided into two parts. The first is the servicing of the car, which means filling it with gas and water, checking oil and tire pressure, and so forth. All this corresponds to the preparatory work of psychosynthesis, the development and cultivation of the various psychological functions and the will-function of the self.

The car is now ready to start. The driver settles himself comfortably in his seat, starts the engine, and operates the appropriate controls for putting the car in motion in the chosen direction. During the trip, the driver steers so as to avoid obstacles, judges when it is possible and safe to pass other vehicles, and decides which road to take at intersections. When he was learning to drive, these operations demanded much conscious attention and effort on his part, but as he became more proficient at them, he performed the mechanics of driving with less and less conscious intervention. This subconscious control is usually described as an automatic process. But this is misleading if the term "automatic" is taken to mean something fixed and rigid; on the contrary, in this case we have intelligent action continuously being modified in accordance with information received by sight, hearing, and kinesthetic data. And fully conscious action can be resumed at any moment, at will, if needed.

The above series of actions corresponds to setting the various psychological functions in motion and directing their operation. Here also there occurs a gradual shifting from a conscious focusing of the full attention on the task to an increasing delegation of responsibility to the unconscious, without the direct intervention of the conscious "I." This process is apparent in the work of acquiring some such technical accomplishment as learning to play a musical instrument. At first, full attention and conscious direction of the execution are demanded. Then, little by little, there comes the formation of what might be called the mechanisms of action, i.e., new neuromuscular patterns. The pianist, for example, now reaches the point at which he no longer needs to pay conscious attention to the mechanics of execution, that is, to directing his fingers to the desired places. He can now give his whole conscious attention to the *quality* of the execution, to the expression of the emotional and aesthetic content of the music that he is performing.

Let us briefly examine how through the will we can use the various psychological functions to reach the goals we have chosen. The methods of doing so vary greatly for each function according to its specific characteristics. Let us consider first of all the use of sensations, of sensory perceptions. Apart from the fact that the limitations inherent in the physical organs of sense permit the perception of only a small part of the impressions and vibrations coming from the external world, our use of these organs is habitually very imperfect and partial: if a sensory perception is to become truly conscious, i.e., "apperceived," it must remain in the *field of consciousness* long enough to be *assimilated* by the conscious "I"; but this field is often cluttered with other psychological contents (sensations of other kinds, emotions, thoughts, etc.). Moreover, the sensory perceptions immediately induce emotional reactions, either positive or negative, which often impede accurate perception and sometimes even misrepresent the object of perception.

The psychology of evidence gives ample proof of this fact. It frequently happens that the depositions of witnesses concerning a given event are either incomplete, or faulty, or both. This occurs even when the deposition is made in good faith and with no conscious attempt to falsify. It is a serious matter which can have grave consequences, such as the conviction of innocent people. When therefore an accurate and objective examination based on precise observation is required, the will must intervene in order to direct, regulate, and use the sensory functions to best advantage.

To do this, it must keep consciousness concentrated on the task of receiving, assimilating, and integrating the messages brought in by the senses. Moreover, it must refuse to acknowledge, for as long as may be necessary, the other sensory impressions, emotions, and mental activities that tend to interfere with the ongoing chosen task. This demands the training of the *power of observation* by means of observation exercises such as those described in *Psychosynthesis.* As we have seen in the story of Agassiz and the fish, major scientists, and especially the naturalists among them, have possessed and further developed by practice this power of observation as promoted and sustained by the will.

The ways in which the will can make use of emotions and feelings as means of realizing its purposes are more complex. First of all, attention and concentration, which are specific functions of the will, must be exercised and strengthened. The nature and intensity of specific emotional energies suggest the best methods of utilizing them. Fundamentally, it is a matter of connecting and relating these energies to the objective to be reached, that is to say, of orienting or channeling the flow of the emotions and feelings toward the predetermined goal. This often requires a transmutation or sublimation of these energies, which in turn involves the will's capacity to engage and direct these energies toward future activities, toward constructive and higher objectives.

I have already discussed the subject of transmutation and sublimation of the sexual and combative energies. Here I may add that this process is based on the close reciprocal action between emotions and feelings on one side and desires and drives on the other. Every painful emotion and feeling arouses the desire and urge to eliminate its cause. Conversely, pleasant and happy emotions prompt the perpetuation of what has produced them. The will can take advantage of this fact to orient, direct, and transmute desires and drives.

All this is valid, however, only for cases in which the emotions, drives, and desires are not excessively intense and respond more or less rapidly and easily to the action of the will. But at times their intensity is such as to arouse resistance, or even a state of violent rebellion against the direction that the will tries to impart to them. Here the will must employ other methods, for if it sets itself in *direct* opposition to those energies, it frequently fails. And even if it does succeed in controlling them by an act of imposition, it arouses conflicts that are wasteful of energy and can have harmful consequences. In these cases, the will's first task is to discharge the intense and excessive tensions of the emotional and propulsive energies. This can be done by means of the various *ventilating* techniques (catharsis), symbolic satisfaction, and, if appropriate, a measure of actual gratification. In this way the will can succeed in eliminating opposition, or in reducing it to a lower level of intensity, so that the energies can now be used in the manner first mentioned. Naturally, no instrument, no "psychic voltmeter," exists for measuring the potential of emotional and impulsive charges, but introspection and observation of spontaneous manifestations can give an approximate idea of their intensity.

The "energy charge" of the will itself must also be reckoned with. A weak will has difficulty in directing emotions even if they are of low or medium intensity, whereas a strong will can do it successfully. The energy relationship between the will and the resistance offered by the psychological material which the will wants to control, direct, and transform must be given proper consideration. Here, experimentation is useful. The strength of the will can be ascertained by definite exercises and experiments in the use of the techniques of direction, transmutation, and sublimation.

There is another psychological function which has close connections with these already mentioned; it is the *imagination.* Here also there are relationships of reciprocal action and reaction. Emotions and desires evoke images which correspond to them. In their turn, the activities of the imagination arouse emotions, desires, and urges. Great is the power of images, and they can be said to constitute a necessary intermediary between the will and the other psychological functions. The dynamic relations between all these functions have been formulated in some of the laws described in the chapter on the skillful will.

The will can learn to direct the imagination to a considerable extent; to achieve this, systematic exercises and training are very helpful. First are exercises in reproductive imagination, using visualization, the evocation of sounds, and memories of sensory impressions in the other sense modalities. One then proceeds to exercises in self-directed creative imagination by starting with a symbol or with an appropriately selected situation. In these exercises, it is the subject's will that substitutes for the therapist, who normally would conduct these exercises in the fashion of Desoille's *guided daydream* and Leuner's *guided affective imagery*. This is not easy, but it can be done. The techniques of the ideal model and of training the imagination, described in *Psychosynthesis*, are useful not only for their own specific purposes, but also for putting the imagination at the behest of and under the direction of the will.

Let us now see how the will can utilize the mind in directing the execution. In the preceding stages, the will has already used the mind as an organ of thought, reflection, foresight, and appropriate programing. In this stage, the direction of the execution, it can and must also use the mind in other ways. When there is a problem to be solved, for which the will has resolved to reach a solution, it focuses the mind's attention on the problem, examines it, reflects upon it, and formulates hypotheses about possible solutions. These hypotheses may subsequently be put to the test of experiment. This can be called "deep thinking" or "reflective meditation" (see Appendix Two, "Thinking and Meditation," page 218).

Another of the mind's functions which can and must be directed by the will is the *intuition*. This leads to the examination of the relations between *will* and *intuition*. It seems evident that the will possesses no *direct* power over the intuitive function; it can even hamper its functioning. But here also the will can perform a most helpful *indirect* action; it can create and keep clear the channel of communication along which the intuitive impressions descend. It does this by imposing a temporary check on the distracting activities of the other psychological functions.

The will can encourage—(encourage, not coerce, I repeat)—the intuitive operation by formulating questions to be addressed to the superconscious sphere, the seat of the intuition. These questions must be given a clear and precise form. The replies may come promptly, but more often they appear after a lapse of time and when least expected (see Appendix Two, page 218).

Part Three
Epilogue

17

THE JOYOUS WILL

The association of will with joy may seem surprising because the will has generally been considered something stern, exacting, forbidding, denying, particularly since the Victorian period.

Yet the "act of willing" can be and often is intrinsically joyous. In order to realize this, it is necessary to have a clear conception of the nature and the various aspects and manifestations of joy. But there is not yet a *coherent psychology of joy,* because a scientific psychology of what Maslow aptly calls "the farther reaches of human nature" of Being-values, or even of true health, is only now in the process of emerging.

The "pursuit of happiness" is considered and is proclaimed in the American Constitution as a right, but rarely is a clear definition given as to what "happiness" means. It is understood in various and divergent ways by different individuals and groups.

It would be well worth while to develop a science and technique of "enjoyment." Maslow hinted at this when, speaking of the Being-values, he said, "Why *not* a technology of joy, of happiness?" Elsewhere, he lists among the Being-values fun, joy, gaiety, and humor.

While it is not possible on this occasion to give the "psychology of joy" its due, a preliminary clarification can be offered for the better understanding of "the joy of willing."

One can say that *"enjoyment" is the concomitant and the result of the satisfaction of a need—of any need.* Thus for each of the levels of needs described by Maslow, there is a corresponding kind of enjoyment. The result of the satisfaction of the *basic* needs can be called *pleasure*. The general subjective state of a person whose "normal" needs and desires are—at least temporarily—satisfied can be called *happiness*.

The result of the fulfillment of the *higher* needs is *joy*. The good will is joyous! It creates a harmonious, joyful atmosphere, and acts of good will have rich and sometimes amazing results. Altruistic, humanitarian activities give deep satisfaction and a sense of fulfilling one's true purpose in life. As an Eastern sage has said, "World tasks are like fires of joy." Finally, the full Transpersonal Self-Realization and even more the communion or identification with universal transcendent Reality has been called *bliss*.

At this point, it is important to recognize that there is no fundamental incompatibility between the satisfaction of all these needs and the consequent "enjoyment." Enjoyment of the higher needs does not exclude enjoyment at all other levels.

There might be and there often are conflicts, crises of adjustment and growth. But they are *temporary* stages in the process of growth, of self-actualization and Self-Realization.

Because of the multiplicity of human nature, of the existence in us of various and often conflicting subpersonalities, joy at some level can coexist with suffering at other levels. For instance, there can be the joy of mastering an unruly subpersonality, although the subpersonality itself may experience this as painful. Also a vivid anticipation of a future willed achievement or satisfaction can give joy even while one feels pain. Saint Francis said, "So great is the Good that I am expecting that every pain to me is joyous." At a less exalted level, this is true of athletes and particularly of mountainclimbers, to whom the joyous prospect of the "intended" willed achievement outweighs the physical hardships and suffering involved.

Since the outcome of successful willing is the satisfaction of one's needs, we can see that the act of will is essentially joyous. And the realization of the self, or more exactly of *being a self* (whose most intrinsic function, as we have seen, is that of willing), gives a sense of freedom, of power, of mastery which is profoundly joyous.

This is true at the level of the personal self; but the realization of the Transpersonal Will, the expression of the Transpersonal Self, is so intensely joyous that it can be called blissful. Here we have the joy of the harmonious union between the personal and the Transpersonal Will; the joy of the harmony between one's Transpersonal Will and those of others; and, highest and foremost, the bliss of the identification with the Universal Will.

The mystics of all times and places have realized and expressed the joy and bliss which are inherent in the union of the individual will with the Universal Will. Underhill says:

> The enhanced will, made over to the interests of the Transcendent, receives new worlds to conquer, new strengths to

match its exalted destiny. But the heart too here enters on a new order, begins to live upon high levels of joy: that is, the sea of delight, the stream of divine influences.

This consummation is vividly expressed in the Sanskrit saying *Sat-Chit-Ananda*: "The blissful awareness of Reality." And finally in the triumphant affirmation: *Aham evam param Brahman*: "I indeed am the Supreme Brahman."

THE WILL
PROJECT

INTRODUCTION TO THE WILL PROJECT

As I noted in the Preface, this volume should be considered as a beginning, and not as an end. The resources of the human will are immense and the purpose of this project is to help in actualizing them.

A very important and urgent application of the use of the will is that concerning the great issue of peace and war. In my view, no amount of political agreements and treaties or of external manipulation can by itself ensure a lasting peace. Many such political agreements and treaties have proved futile. As it is stated so aptly in the preamble to the constitution of UNESCO, "Since wars begin in the minds of men, it is in the minds of men that the defenses of peace must be constructed."

The effective means to change men's inner attitude, both individual and collective, is the constant application of good will. It would have the effect of a magic wand. Expressed and applied, good will automatically excludes violent conflicts and wars. It would be well to realize this strategic point and to make a campaign for good will, in schools and everywhere, a major concern.

Of course, there are even higher uses of the will. The Transpersonal Will and the unification with the Universal Will can add a still greater incentive and means for the achieving of true peace.

The following program is intended as a preliminary map for further exploration of the will. It can be expanded and modified. It is a *basis* for future work which can yield enormous rewards.

An international group is gradually being formed to act as a focal point and to pool the responses and experiences of all who wish to take an active part in the Will Project. This information will subsequently be used in another book planned to deal with the practical applications of the will in many different areas of activity, especially psychology and education.

While this group is being organized, answers to the questionnaire (see Appendix Three, pages 233–34) and reports of work and experiences from all English-language countries can be addressed to:

> Psychosynthesis Institute,
> 150 Doherty Way,
> Redwood City,
> California 94062,
> U.S.A.

For Italian-, French-, and German-speaking areas, correspondence can be addressed to:

> Istituto di Psicosintesi,
> Via San Domenico, 16,
> 50133, Firenze,
> Italy.

WILL PROJECT

Program of Research on the Will and Its Applications

Outline

I. *History of the Theories, Beliefs, and Doctrines on the Will*

II. *The Will in Modern Psychology*

III. *Nature and Aspects of the Will*
1. Strong Will
2. Skillful Will
3. Good Will
4. Transpersonal Will
5. Individual Will identified with the Universal Will

IV. *Qualities of the Will*
1. Energy—Dynamic Power—Intensity
2. Mastery—Control—Discipline
3. Concentration—Attention—One-Pointedness—Focus
4. Determination—Decisiveness—Resoluteness—Promptness
5. Persistence—Endurance—Patience
6. Initiative—Courage—Daring
7. Organization—Integration—Synthesis

V. *Stages of the Volitional Act*
1. Purpose—Aim—Goal—Valuation—Motivation—Intention
2. Deliberation
3. Choice—Decision
4. Affirmation—Command

5. Planning and Programing
6. Direction of the Execution

VI. *Relationships of the Will with the Other Psychological Functions*
Sensory-Motor—Impulses—Drives and Desire—Emotions and Feelings—Imagination—Thought—Intuition

VII. *Methods for the Development and Training of the Will*
1. Physical Activities: Manual labor—Gymnastics—Rhythmic movements—Sport
2. "Useless" exercises
3. Training the Will in daily life
4. Use of External Aids: Words and phrases—Images—Music
5. Concentration—Meditation—Invocation
6. Affirmation—Command
7. Creative activities

VIII. *Fields of Application of the Will*
1. Individual:
   a. Psychotherapy
   b. Education
   c. Self-actualization (Personal psychosynthesis)
   d. Self-realization and Spiritual psychosynthesis
2. Interpersonal and Social relationships
   a. Between two individuals
   b. Family group
   c. Communities and social groups of various kinds
   d. Racial groups
   e. Religious groups

f. National groups

g. International relationships

3. Planetary relationships (ecology); between the four kingdoms of nature: Mineral—Vegetable—Animal—Human

4. Relationship between the human will and the Universal Will

IX. *Experimentation*

By individuals and groups—reports of results

X. *Collections of Examples of the Use of the Will and Its Results*

1. Historical figures

2. Individuals

a. Self-actualizing

b. Self-realizing

c. Clients

d. Pupils

XI. *Bibliography on the Will*

In various languages

XII. *Specific Projects*

1. By individuals

2. By groups

....

Organization and Execution of the Program Through:

I. *Foundations—Institutes—Centers—Groups*

1. For the whole program

2. For specialized research, experimentation, and application. Location and fields of work: local—national—according to language areas

II. *Communication and Diffusion*
Through: Lectures—Publications (articles—pamphlets—books—international journals)—Conferences—Symposia—Associations

III. *Coordination and Utilization*

Appendices

APPENDIX ONE

SELF-IDENTIFICATION
EXERCISE

DISIDENTIFICATION AND
SELF-IDENTIFICATION

We are dominated by everything with which our self becomes identified. We can dominate, direct, and utilize everything from which we disidentify ourselves.

The central, fundamental experience of self-consciousness, the discovery of the "I," is implicit in our human consciousness.* It is that which distinguishes our consciousness from that of the animals, which are conscious but not self-conscious. But generally this self-consciousness is indeed "implicit" rather than explicit. It is experienced in a nebulous and distorted way because it is usually mixed with and veiled by the *contents* of consciousness.

This constant input of influences veils the clarity of consciousness and produces spurious identifications of the self with the content of consciousness, rather than with consciousness

* "Self-consciousness" is used here in the purely psychological sense of being aware of oneself as a distinct individual and not in the customary sense of egocentric and even neurotic "self-centeredness."

itself. If we are to make self-consciousness explicit, clear, and vivid, we must first *dis*identify ourselves from the contents of our consciousness.

More specifically, the habitual state for most of us is to be identified with that which seems, at any one time, to give us the greatest sense of aliveness, which seems to us to be most real, or most intense.

This identification with a part of ourselves is usually related to the predominant function or focus of our awareness, to the predominant role we play in life. It can take many forms. Some people are identified with their bodies. They experience themselves, and often talk about themselves, mainly in terms of sensation; in other words they function as if they *were* their bodies. Others are identified with their feelings; they experience and describe their state of being in affective terms, and believe their feelings to be the central and most intimate part of themselves, while thoughts and sensations are perceived as more distant, perhaps somewhat separate. Those who are identified with their minds are likely to describe themselves with intellectual constructs, even when asked how they *feel.* They often consider feelings and sensations as peripheral, or are largely unaware of them. Many are identified with a role, and live, function, and experience themselves *in terms of that role,* such as "mother," "husband," "wife," "student," "businessman," "teacher," etc.

This identification with only *a part* of our personality may be temporarily satisfactory, but it has serious drawbacks. It prevents us from realizing the experience of the "I," the deep sense of self-identification, of knowing who we are. It excludes, or greatly decreases, the ability to identify with all the other parts of our personality, to enjoy them and utilize them to their full extent. Thus our "normal" expression in the world is limited at any one time to only a fraction of what it can be. The conscious—or even unconscious—realization that we somehow do not have access to much that is in us can cause frustration and painful feelings of inadequacy and failure.

Finally, a continuing identification with either a role or a predominant function leads often, and almost inevitably, to a precarious life situation resulting sooner or later in a sense of loss, even despair, such as in the case of an athlete who grows old and loses his physical strength; an actress whose physical beauty is fading; a mother whose children have grown up and left her; or a student who has to leave school and face a new set of responsibilities. Such situations can produce serious and often very painful crises. They can be considered as more or less partial psychological "deaths." No frantic clinging to the waning old "identity" can avail. The true solution can be only a "rebirth," that is, entering into a new and broader identification. This sometimes involves the whole personality and requires and leads to an awakening or "birth" into a new and higher state of *being*. The process of death and rebirth was symbolically enacted in various mystery rites and has been lived and described in religious terms by many mystics. At present it is being rediscovered in terms of transpersonal experiences and realizations.

This process often occurs without a clear understanding of its meaning and often against the wish and will of the individual involved in it. But a conscious, purposeful, willing cooperation can greatly facilitate, foster, and hasten it.

It can be best done by a deliberate exercise of *disidentification* and *self-identification*. Through it we gain the *freedom* and the *power of choice* to be identified with, or disidentified from, any aspect of our personality, according to what seems to us most appropriate in each situation. Thus we can learn to master, direct, and utilize all the elements and aspects of our personality, in an inclusive and harmonious synthesis. Therefore this exercise is considered as basic in psychosynthesis.

IDENTIFICATION EXERCISE

This exercise is intended as a tool for achieving the consciousness of the self, and the ability to focus our attention sequentially on each of our main personality aspects, roles, etc.

We then become clearly aware of and can examine their qualities while maintaining the point of view of the observer, and recognizing that *the observer is not that which he observes.*

In the form which follows, the first phase of the exercise—the disidentification—consists of three parts dealing with the physical, emotional, and mental aspects of awareness. This leads to the self-identification phase. Once some experience is gained with it, the exercise can be expanded or modified according to need, as will be indicated further on.

Procedure

Put your body in a comfortable and relaxed position, and slowly take a few deep breaths (preliminary exercises of relaxation can be useful). Then make the following affirmation, slowly and thoughtfully:

> "I *have* a body but *I am not* my body. My body may find itself in different conditions of health or sickness, it may be rested or tired, but that has nothing to do with *my self,* my real 'I.' I value my body as my precious instrument of experience and of action in the outer world, but *it is only an instrument.* I treat it well, I seek to keep it in good health, but it is *not* myself. I *have* a body, but I *am not* my body."

Now close your eyes, recall briefly in your consciousness the general substance of this affirmation, and then gradually focus your attention on the central concept: "I *have* a body but I *am not* my body." Attempt, as much as you can, to realize this as an *experienced fact* in your consciousness. Then open your eyes and proceed the same way with the next two stages:

> "I *have* emotions, but I *am not* my emotions. My emotions are diversified, changing, sometimes contradictory. They may swing from love to hatred, from calm to anger, from joy to sorrow, and yet my essence—my true nature—does not change. 'I' remain. Though a wave of anger may temporarily submerge me, I know that it will

pass in time; therefore *I am not* this anger. Since I can observe and understand my emotions, and then gradually learn to direct, utilize, and integrate them harmoniously, it is clear that they are not my *self.* I *have* emotions, but I *am not* my emotions.

"I *have* a mind but I *am not* my mind. My mind is a valuable tool of discovery and expression, but *it is not* the essence of my being. Its contents are constantly changing as it embraces new ideas, knowledge, and experience. Sometimes it refuses to obey me. Therefore, it cannot be me my self. It is *an organ of knowledge* in regard to both the outer and the inner worlds, but it is not *my self.* I *have* a mind, but I *am not* my mind."

Next comes the phase of *identification.* Affirm slowly and thoughtfully:

"After the disidentification of *myself,* the 'I,' from the contents of consciousness, such as sensations, emotions, thoughts, *I recognize and affirm that I am a center of pure self-consciousness.* I am *a center of will,* capable of observing, directing, and using all my psychological processes and my physical body."

Focus your attention on the central realization: *"I am a center of pure self-consciousness and of will."* Attempt, as much as you can, to realize this as an *experienced* fact in your awareness.

As the purpose of the exercise is to achieve a specific state of consciousness, once that purpose is grasped much of the procedural detail can be dispensed with. Thus, after having practiced it for some time—and some might do this from the very beginning—one can modify the exercise by going swiftly and dynamically through each of the stages of disidentification, using only the central affirmation of each stage and concentrating on its *experiential* realization.

I *have* a body, but I *am not* my body.

I *have* emotions, but I *am not* my emotions.

I *have* a mind, but I *am not* my mind.

At this point it is valuable to make a deeper consideration of the stage of self-identification along the following lines:

> "What am I then? What remains after having disidentified myself from my body, my sensations, my feelings, my desires, my mind, my actions? It is the essence of myself—*a center of pure self-consciousness*. It is the permanent factor in the ever varying flow of my personal life. It is that which gives me a sense of being, of permanence, of inner balance. *I affirm my identity with this center* and realize its permanency and its energy.
>
> (pause)
>
> "I recognize and affirm myself as a center of pure self-awareness and of creative, dynamic energy. I realize that from this center of true identity I can learn to observe, direct, and harmonize all the psychological processes and the physical body. I will to achieve a constant awareness of this fact in the midst of my everyday life, and to use it to help me and give increasing meaning and direction to my life."

As the attention is shifted increasingly to the *state of consciousness,* the identification stage also can be abridged. The goal is to gain enough facility with the exercise so that one can go through each stage of disidentification swiftly and dynamically in a short time, and then remain in the "I" consciousness for as long as desired. One can then—*at will,* and at any moment—disidentify from any overpowering emotion, annoying thought, inappropriate role, etc., and from the vantage point of the detached observer gain a clearer understanding of the situation, its meaning, its causes, and the most effective way to deal with it.

This exercise has been found most effective if practiced daily, preferably during the first hours of the day. Whenever possible, it is to be done shortly after waking up and considered as a symbolic *second awakening*. It is also of great value to repeat it in its brief form several times during the day, returning to the state of disidentified "I" consciousness.

The exercise may be modified appropriately, according to one's own purpose and existential needs, by adding stages of disidentification to include other functions besides the three fundamental ones (physical, emotional, mental), as well as subpersonalities, roles, etc. It can also begin with disidentification from material possessions. Some examples follow:

> "I *have* desires, but *I am not* my desires. Desires are aroused by drives, physical and emotional, and by other influences. They are often changeable and contradictory, with alternations of attraction and repulsion; therefore they are not my *self*. I *have* desires, but *I am not* my desires." (This is best placed between the emotional and mental stage.)

> "I engage in various activities and play many roles in life. I must play these roles and I willingly play them as well as possible, be it the role of son or father, wife or husband, teacher or student, artist or executive. But *I am more* than the son, the father, the artist. These are roles, specific but *partial* roles, which I, myself, am playing, agree to play, can watch and observe myself playing. Therefore *I am not* any of them. *I am self-identified*, and I am not only the actor, but *the director* of the acting."

This exercise can be and is being performed very effectively in groups. The group leader voices the affirmations and the members listen with eyes closed, letting the significance of the words penetrate deeply.

APPENDIX TWO

THINKING
AND MEDITATION

As in the case of many other words used in psychology (for example, "mind," "personality," "soul"), different meanings are ascribed to the word "meditation." In its more restricted sense, it can be regarded as synonymous with disciplined thought or reflection on an idea. More broadly, it embraces other kinds of inner action, for which disciplined thought is a prerequisite. In psychosynthesis meditation is considered and practiced in this wider connotation. We shall thus indicate with appropriate terminology, as the need arises, the types of meditation we wish to discuss.

The three principal types are: *reflective meditation; receptive meditation; creative meditation.*

Meditation, to be effective, needs adequate preparation. It is a matter of passing from normal life with its outward orientation, in which interest and attention are monopolized by our concerns, plans, and activities, to the "inner action" of meditation. This preparation is triple: physical, emotional, and mental.

1. *Physical relaxation*—the most thorough elimination possible of all muscular and nervous tension.
2. *Emotional composure*—the endeavor to assume a state of tranquillity.

3. *Mental recollection*—the direction of the mind's interest and attention inward.

I. Reflective Meditation

Its simplest definition is *to think;* an accurate but limited definition, since clear ideas on the function of thinking are not common property. It has been stated that "the mind thinks in us," rather than it being we who formulate thoughts. Indeed, the working of our minds normally proceeds spontaneously under the action of stimuli and interests of various kinds, and in a somewhat disorganized way. The mind operates independently of the will, and often in opposition to it. This lack of mastery over the mind has been well described by Swami Vivekananda:

> How hard it is to control the mind. Well has it been compared to the maddened monkey. There was a monkey, restless by his own nature, as all monkeys are. As if that were not enough, someone made him drink freely of wine, so that he became still more restless. Then a scorpion stung him. When a man is stung by a scorpion he jumps about for the whole day; so the poor monkey found his condition worse than ever. To complete his misery, a demon entered into him. What language can describe the uncontrollable restlessness of that monkey? The human mind is like that monkey; incessantly active by its own nature; then it becomes drunk with the wine of desire, thus increasing its turbulence. After desire takes possession comes the sting of the scorpion of jealousy of the success of others, and last of all the demon of pride enters the mind, making it think itself of all importance. How hard to control such a mind!
>
> The first lesson, then, is to sit for some time and let the mind run on. The mind is bubbling up all the time. It is like that monkey jumping about. Let the monkey jump as much as he can; you simply wait and watch. Knowledge is power, says the proverb, and that is true. Until you

know what the mind is doing you cannot control it. Give it the rein; many hideous thoughts may come into it; you may be astonished that it was possible for you to think such thoughts. But you will find that each day the mind's vagaries are becoming less and less violent, that each day it is becoming calmer. In the first few months you will find that the mind will have a great many thoughts, later you will find that they have somewhat decreased, and in a few more months they will be fewer and fewer, until at last the mind will be under perfect control, but we must patiently practise every day.

Much of our ordinary mental activity, then, does not merit the term "thought." It is only when a dominating interest backed by a firm and decided will is able to hold the mind concentrated on an idea or task that it really "thinks" and we can say that it reflects, it meditates. Thus there are those who meditate without calling their mental activity that; for example, the scientist seeking the solution to a problem; the businessman working out a program for the conduct of his affairs. This is a regulated and organized use of the thinking function. In this connection we should recognize a somewhat humiliating truth: these people frequently think and meditate much more efficiently than those who try to do so for psychological or spiritual purposes.

If we want to learn to meditate, we must realize that the mind is in reality an "instrument," an inner tool from which we must disidentify ourselves if we are to make use of it at will. While we are wholly identified with the mind, we cannot control it. A certain "psychological distance," a certain detachment from it, is needed.

The practice of *concentration* is the first step; the next is to direct the activity of the mind along a line we have determined, so that it accomplishes the task we have assigned to it. In this sense to "think" means to reflect on and deeply explore a subject, examining all its implications, ramifications, and meanings. An attempt on our part to do this will quickly reveal how superficial and inadequate is our normal way of "thinking." We are accustomed to reach hurried conclusions and arbitrary generalizations, to consider only *one aspect* of the subject, and to see or accentuate only what corresponds to our preconceptions or preferences.

The first requisite for developing the art of thinking is to watch carefully the process of thinking itself and be instantly aware when a deviation starts. The second involves *persistence,* tenacity in probing deeply into the subject. Here a curious phenomenon occurs; a few minutes of reflection seem to have exhausted the possibilities of the subject; nothing further remains to be said about it. But persistence in reflection at this point will lead to the discovery of other, unsuspected aspects, revealing a wealth of development to which we can ascribe no limits.

An example will serve to make this clear. Let us take as a theme for meditation the sentence "I seek to love, not hate." At first sight this appears simple and evident, indeed banal, and makes one think, "Naturally, being a good person, with good intentions, I try to love and not hate; it's so obvious that I can't find anything else to add." But if we ask ourselves—and attempt to answer—the following questions, we shall realize that the matter is not so simple. "What does love really mean? —What is love? —How many and what kinds of love are there? —In what ways am I capable of loving? —How do I try to love? —Whom do I love and whom do I *succeed* in loving? —Have I always succeeded in loving as I would have wished? —If not, why? —What have been and are the obstacles and how can I eliminate them? —What portion of my love depends on the people to whom it is directed and what on my own nature?"

Then we can examine the word "hate," and come up with such questions as: "Behind what camouflage can it hide? —Am I free from every type of hate? Do I feel hate toward those who injure me? —Toward those hostile to me? —Are such feelings fair? —If not, how can they be corrected? —What attitude should be adopted toward evil in general? —What is the meaning of the saying 'An enemy is as useful as a Buddha?' " *

It is obvious that we cannot examine all these queries in one meditation. They offer possibilities for reflection for an extended series of meditations. Thus we discover what a wealth of possible elaboration, how much meaning, is concealed in such a seemingly simple statement.

What are the aims of meditation? We must be clear about them, for they determine the theme to be chosen and the procedure to be adopted. One of the objects of reflective meditation is conceptual, that is, to have a clear idea about the given subject or problem. Clarity of concept is much rarer than is supposed, and the first step here also is to become aware that our ideas are not clear. Another object, more important still, is to acquire *knowledge about ourselves* (we will speak of this later).

Some subjects for meditation are:

1. The various psychological and spiritual qualities we desire to awaken or strengthen in ourselves: *courage, faith, serenity, joy, will,* etc.

2. Symbols. (See the extensive discussion of symbols and their uses in *Psychosynthesis.*)

3. A sentence expressing a thought—this has been termed a "seed-thought"—of which there are two principal categories:

* A word of warning is in order concerning meditation on negative subjects. A fundamental aspect of meditation consists in intensely focusing our attention on the subject chosen for meditation. This energizes and magnifies it, because of the "feeding power of attention" (see Practical Applications of the Skillful Will: Psychological Breathing and Feeding, page 69). So direct meditation on a negative subject must definitely be avoided. However, meditation on a negative aspect can be *safe* and *useful* provided it is done *in a positive way*, that is for the purpose of, and with our *interest* resolutely focused on, improving the condition, or reducing or neutralizing that which is negative. The approach to "hate," described above, is an example of this positive approach.

But such meditation is a relatively advanced undertaking. It is best to attempt it after having developed considerable proficiency and control, and only when a definite and specific need arises.

a. Those that seem simple and obvious, like the one we have commented on ("I seek to love . . .").

b. Those that, on the contrary, are formulated in such a paradoxical way as to be perplexing at first. Their form is built on apparent contradictions, which can be reconciled only by finding a synthesis at a higher and more comprehensive level. The koans of Zen Buddhism are extreme types of these paradoxical seed-thoughts. Here are some instances of some paradoxes, which could be called psychospiritual quizzes: "To act with interest and disinterest"—"To suffer with joy" (which does not mean to enjoy suffering)—"To make haste slowly"—"To live in the eternal and the moment"—"To see action in inaction and inaction in action" (the theme of one of the books of the *Bhagavad Gita*).

4. The most important, indeed, the indispensable, subject for meditation in achieving personal psychosynthesis is reflective meditation on one's self. By means of it one is able to distinguish between pure self-consciousness or awareness of the SELF and the psychological elements or parts of one's personality at various levels. This distinction has already been spoken of, but your attention is recalled to it because it is a fundamental requisite for acquiring consciousness of the SELF.

This awareness, this possibility of observing one's own personality "from above" and "from a distance interiorly," should not be confused with egocentricity and preoccupation with self. These in reality reflect just the opposite, being *identification* with the personality elements and concern with personal defects and the opinions and judgments of others about ourselves, which often arouse an acute sense of distress.

Finally, reflective meditation on ourselves is not to be considered simply a passive process of observation, like making an inventory of facts. It aims at *understanding, interpretation,* and *evaluation* of what we discover in ourselves.*

---

* Another word of caution is needed here. Meditation on ourselves can at times cause the emergence in consciousness of disturbing personality elements, or the

II. Receptive Meditation

A clear understanding of the difference between reflective and receptive meditation can be more easily gained by regarding the mind as an "inner eye." In reflective meditation, the mind's eye is directed, so to speak, horizontally. It observes the object, the theme of the meditation, the seed-thought, or the various aspects of the personality. In receptive meditation, on the other hand, the mind's eye is turned upwards, seeking to discover what is to be discerned at a higher level than that of the ordinary consciousness and of the mind itself.

The first stage is *silence*. The reception from the superconscious of an intuition, an inspiration, a message, or a stimulus to action requires the elimination of what might impede its descent into the sphere of consciousness. This is why silence is necessary. In this connection, a person accustomed to meditating has reported the following experience:

> I was immersed in a profound meditation and knew that I had reached a limpid, radiant state, when this thought crossed my mind: "I know I am at this level, and yet I am deaf and blind and can hear and see nothing." A moment passed and then this humorous reply came: "If you were silent as well, you would be able to see and hear."

To keep and maintain inner silence entails continuous effort; the mind is not accustomed to this discipline; it kicks against the pricks and tries to escape.

There are various ways of obtaining mastery over the mind. The first, indicated by Vivekananda, consists in maintaining

increasing presence of negative emotions. If this occurs, it is because the meditation was done incorrectly, that is, not from a sufficiently objective, disidentified point. But maintaining such a poised point in consciousness is particularly hard when meditating on ourselves, and at first may be too difficult or even impossible for some of us, such as the more introspective or imaginative types. When this is the case it is advisable to postpone meditating on ourselves, and for a time to choose more impersonal topics while also putting much emphasis on the practice of disidentification.

the steady, patient attitude of the observer for a certain time, until the mind tires of its restless activity. This can be practiced, patiently, for a short period each day. Another method consists in persistently repeating a word or phrase, murmuring the words aloud. A third way is to evoke a mental picture. The most effective words and pictures are those that induce a state of calm, peace, and silence. An appropriate phrase is one taken from a hymn of the Greek Mysteries: "Be silent, O strings, that a new melody may flow in me." Effective pictures include a tranquil lake which mirrors the blue of the sky; a majestic mountaintop; and especially, the starry sky in the silence of the night.

In other cases the opposite difficulty arises: a sense of heaviness or somnolence comes on. This is to be strenuously resisted, since it may lead to a state of passivity in which elements erupt from the unconscious, particularly from the lower and collective unconscious, or from extraneous psychic energies. As soon as one is aware of this happening, the condition must be interrupted and the meditation suspended, at least for a while. In general, receptive meditation presents greater difficulties than reflective meditation, and its practice must be vigilantly conducted if damaging effects are to be avoided.

How and in what form do the "messages" come, that is, the material we "receive"? The most common way is by *vision* or *illumination*. As has been said, the mind is symbolically an "inner eye," and therefore it can "see" in the sense of *understand*. It can become aware of the meaning of facts and events, "see" the solution of a problem and have a "luminous" idea.

Intuition is a higher form of vision. Etymologically, it is related to vision and means to "see within" (*in-tueri*). At its highest it can be equated with a direct suprarational comprehension of the nature of reality, of its essence. It thus differs from what is commonly called "intuition" (hunches, psychic impressions, presentiments concerning people and events).

The inner action of one who is endeavouring to perceive inner reality is called "contemplation" or the "contemplative state." The highest form of inner vision is *illumination*, which can be defined as revelation of the divinity inherent in all things, in nature and in living beings.

A second effect of receptive meditation may be "inner hearing"; but here also it is necessary to discriminate carefully between the psychic perception of voices and sounds and true transpersonal hearing. The information coming from the higher levels is for the most part impersonal in character; the messages are brief, but pregnant with meaning. They often have a symbolic quality, even when they appear to carry a concrete meaning. A well-known example is the message received by Saint Francis: "Go and restore my Church." Initially he interpreted this as an injunction to rebuild a little ruined church. Later he understood that he had been asked something very different, to restore the Church itself, which was in decline in his time. Many artistic, literary, and musical impressions belong in this category of inner hearing.

Sometimes a veritable dialogue occurs between the personal "I" and the Self. The mind, recollected in meditation, refers questions and receives inner replies, rapid and clear. When attempting such a dialogue, however, much prudence and discrimination must be exercised. Not infrequently "voices" are experienced and "messages" are received which come from or are transmitted by the personal or collective unconscious, and whose contents do not tally with truth. They can deceive and are apt to dominate and obsess.

A third form of receptivity may be termed "contact," since it has a certain resemblance to the sense of touch or "feeling by contact." It conveys a meaning similar to the content of the phrases "to establish contact with somebody," "to be *en rapport* with someone." It is an inner contact, one with the Self. It indicates a relationship, liaison, or alignment with the Self which renders us receptive to its quality, enabling us to identify or unify ourselves consciously, even if only for a moment, with that spiritual reality. This inner nearness, this "touch" of the Self, harmonizes, vivifies, and recharges us with energy.

The fourth way of receiving an impression from the higher Self takes the form of a *stimulus to action;* our awareness of it arouses in us the urge to do a given thing, embark upon a particular activity, or assume certain duties and tasks.

The reception is followed by the stage of *registration*; that is, a phase in which a clear awareness of what has been received is reached and that awareness is *maintained.* It is advisable to record immediately in writing what has been perceived. Impressions of high origin are often vivid and clear *at the moment,* but are apt to vanish rapidly from the field of consciousness and if not caught and recorded immediately, are often lost. Moreover, the mere fact of fixing them in written terms contributes to a better understanding of them; even more, the impression sometimes develops while we write, so that, in a certain sense, we continue to "receive."

Another interesting kind of receptivity is *delayed reception.* It frequently happens that during receptive meditation nothing seems to occur and we remain in a state of "darkness." Nothing new appears on the surface of consciousness except a general sense of calm and repose. But this does not necessarily mean that the meditation has been fruitless. Often, during the day or the following days, an impression or inspiration presents itself unexpectedly. It can come at any moment while one is engaged in some completely different activity, or in moments of repose, or on awaking in the morning. Sometimes one can trace the relationship between the apparently unsuccessful meditation and the subsequent inspiration. Therefore after the close of a meditation we should maintain an inner attitude of watchful waiting, definable as "the meditative attitude," which, when developed by exercise, can be persisted in more or less throughout the day. We can thus train ourselves to hold a state of double awareness; this implies the ability to concentrate normally on our outer activities and keep a part of the attention directed toward the inner world.

I would offer, also, these *technical suggestions on meditation*:

Cease meditating for a time whenever overstimulation or its symptoms occur: nervous tension, emotional excitement, feverish activity. The length of time to be spent on meditation varies, but to begin with, it should not exceed ten or fifteen minutes; that is quite long enough. The period during which one subject should be used as the theme also varies, but it should not be less than a week, and after some practice one often finds a month too short. Some subjects appear to be virtually inexhaustible! A good method is to meditate on a series of themes in rotation, one theme to be used each week until the series is gone through again. Finally, there is one way of practicing receptive meditation that offers many advantages. Group meditation helps concentration (with few exceptions), confers a mutual integration and protection, and, moreover, makes possible a reciprocal verification and sharing of each member's results.

III. Creative Meditation

Meditation can be creative because it is "inner action." A contrast is sometimes made between meditation and action, but this is erroneous. The mastery and application of psychological and spiritual energies *are* actions, for they require will, training, and the employment of appropriate techniques; and above all because they are effective—they produce results.

There are various purposes for which we can use creative meditation. The first and most important is *self-creation*. By means of meditation we can modify, transform, and regenerate our personality. One effective way of doing this is the "ideal model" exercise (see *Psychosynthesis*). It may be regarded as a "model" of creative meditation.

We are using the creative power of thought and all other psychological forces continuously, spontaneously, and, I would say, inevitably. But usually we do so without being aware of it, haphazardly, and thus with little constructive effect or at worst with definite injury to ourselves and others.

A beneficial application demands above all that we ascertain the *motives* that animate us, and that we accord passage only to the good ones, that is, those which are the expression of the "will-to-good." It is then necessary to determine our objectives precisely. In the present period of reconstruction new "forms" are being built in every sphere of life, and we can cooperate by assisting in the creation and manifestation of the ideas that inform, animate, and mold these new forms.

The various stages of creative meditation are:

1. Clear conception and precise formulation of the idea;

2. Use of the imagination, i.e., "clothing" of the idea in pictures and "suggestive" symbols;

3. Vivifying the idea with warmth of feeling and the propulsive force of desire.

An extensive outline of a meditation on the will is given below. The same pattern, with suitable modifications, can be used for other subjects. It can also be adapted according to the specific aim as well as the psychological type of the meditator.

OUTLINE OF MEDITATION ON THE WILL

I. *Preparation*

1. *Psychical Relaxation, Emotional Composure, Mental Recollection*

2. *Concentration*
   Realization of the point of pure self-awareness

3. *Elevation*
   Directing the aspiration of the heart and the attention of mind toward the SELF

4. *Identification*

Imaginative and affirmative identification with the
SELF

II. *Reflective Meditation*
Suggested Themes:

1. *One of the Stages of the Volitional Act*
Purpose—Aim—Goal—Valuation—Motivation—
Intention
Deliberation
Choice—Decision
Affirmation—Command
Planning and Programing
Direction of the Execution

2. *One of the Qualities of the Will*
Energy—Dynamic Power—Intensity
Mastery—Control—Discipline
Concentration—Attention—One-Pointedness—Focus
Determination—Decisiveness—Resoluteness—
Promptness
Persistence—Endurance—Patience
Initiative—Courage—Daring
Organization—Integration—Synthesis

III. *Use of Symbols*

1. *Visualization*
Visualize vividly and steadily a symbol of the Will.
Suggested images:
a) A flaming torch
b) Moses (by Michelangelo)
c) A charioteer holding the reins of three horses
(Krishna in the *Bhagavad Gita*)
d) A man at the helm of a boat
e) An orchestra conductor conducting

2. *Auditory Symbols*
Suggested sound: Siegfried's Motive (by Wagner)

IV. *Receptive Meditation*

1. *Appeal*
"Let the Will of the SELF guide and direct my life."

2. *Reception*

Silent realization of the downflow of the Will energy into the personality, at all levels (mental—emotional —physical).

V. *Affirmation*

"I proclaim and celebrate the Will in thought and word and deed."

VI. *Expression*

1. Say aloud: "The Will-to-Good of the SELF expresses itself in me as good will."
2. Choose and formulate some definite use of the Will to be demonstrated in daily life.

APPENDIX THREE

QUESTIONNAIRE
ON THE WILL

A general questionnaire for self-assessment and self-knowledge is contained in the chapter on General Assessment in *Psychosynthesis*, pages 78–84. While written primarily for therapeutic purposes, it can be used with little modification for self-actualization and for educational psychosynthesis.

The following Questionnaire on the Will is intended primarily as a self-survey to be made after reading this book, and can also be of definite value in psychotherapy and educational settings. It constitutes an important part of the general assessment, which is a necessary preliminary stage to individual psychosynthesis. It has specific value and meets a real need—to ascertain the strengths, weaknesses, and complexities of the will-function. It can serve as a solid basis for establishing an effective and balanced program for training the will. Training the will is a lifetime task and requires persistence, patience, steady intention, and purposiveness. Results come from a conscientiously applied program, well repaying the effort and making further work increasingly easy. Written answers to the questionnaire are useful in various ways and can be profitably renewed at determined intervals, as a check on progress and a spur to action.

QUESTIONNAIRE ON THE WILL

I. *Aspects of the Will* (Strong, Skillful, Good, Transpersonal)
Which are more developed and active in you?
Which are little developed or undeveloped?

II. *Qualities of the Will* (Energy—Dynamic Power—Intensity; Mastery—Control—Discipline; Concentration—Attention—One-Pointedness—Focus; Determination—Decisiveness—Resoluteness—Promptness; Persistence—Endurance—Patience; Initiative—Courage—Daring; Organization—Integration—Synthesis)
Which are developed and active
1. slightly?
2. in a fairly balanced way?
3. *relatively* too much (in comparison with the others)?

III. *Stages of the Will* (Purpose—Aim—Goal—Valuation—Motivation—Intention; Deliberation; Decision—Choice; Affirmation—Command; Planning and Programing; Direction of the Execution)
1. Which stages of the will are more developed and functioning better in you?
2. Which are undeveloped?
3. Which are *relatively* overdeveloped (in comparison with the others)?

IV. *Training and Active Development of the Will*
1. Have you done exercises for training the will? Which? With what results?
2. Which exercises are you doing at present? Which do you intend to do in the future?

V. What influences (external and inner) have helped you in developing and using the will?
What influences (external and inner) have hindered you in developing and using the will?

VI. Have you any suggestions, facts, or observations to communicate about the will? Can you quote examples or experiences (historic or private) of the use and development of the will? *

VII. Have you any other comments to make or questions to ask about the will?

* See Introduction to the Will Project, page 203.

APPENDIX FOUR

HISTORICAL SURVEY

When we approach the subject of the will, we are faced with a peculiar, even a paradoxical, situation. We find that in the past, and approximately up to the beginning of this century, the will has been the object of widespread interest among philosophers, theologians, educators, and some psychologists with a philosophical turn of mind.

A historical account and discussion of the many, often contrasting, concepts of the will lie outside the scope of this survey. These concepts constitute one of the objectives of the research advocated in the Will Project outlined above.

Yet it seems appropriate, in the interests of providing a perspective and a framework, to indicate briefly some of the more significant views of those who have dealt with the subject of the will. In India, the Raja Yoga method of psychological and spiritual development stresses the need of using the will. In Patanjali's *Yoga Sutras*, we read:

> The control of these modifications of the mind is to be brought about through tireless endeavor, and through non-attachment.
>
> When the object to be gained is sufficiently valued, and the efforts towards its attainment are persistently followed without intermission, then the steadiness of the mind is secured.

The attainment of this stage (spiritual consciousness) is rapid for those whose will is intensely alive.

Those who employ the will likewise differ, for its use may be intense, moderate or gentle.

According to Patanjali, "one of the siddhis, or psychic powers, the Yogin has to develop is *irresistible will* (prakamya)."

The great importance attributed by Zen Buddhism to the will is reflected in the following statements by D. T. Suzuki:

> . . . the most important fact that lies behind the experience of enlightenment, therefore, is that the Buddha made the most strenuous attempt to solve the problem of Ignorance and his utmost will-power was brought to bear upon a successful issue of the struggle. . . . Enlightenment therefore must involve *the will as well as the intellect.* . . .
>
> The Will is the man himself and Zen appeals to it.

Europe has had its voluntaristic schools of thought, which assigned to the will a central position in man. Augustine stated that man and God are nothing else than will (*Nihil aliud quam voluntates sunt*). Duns Scotus, the outstanding representative of the voluntaristic theological school, asserted that "the nature of the soul is will." Leibniz can be regarded as one of the pioneers in upholding a dynamic conception of the psychological life. He emphasized purpose as the basic characteristic of the will and maintained that purpose and activity are basic in mental life (*Quod non agit non existit*).

Later voluntaristic conceptions were held and expounded by such philosophers as Fichte, Schelling, Von Hartmann, and Nietzsche. But the very broad conceptions of the "will" they put forward embraced all kinds of "conations," as well as an "unconscious will," and therefore did not recognize the specific characteristic of *human* will, that is, *conscious* choice.

In France, several philosophers have discussed the will. Outstanding among them was Maine de Biran, according to whom the will manifests as an *effort* to surmount resistances principally created by the body and the desires, and is the direct expression of the I (*moi*). Others who recognized the primacy of the will were Sécretant, Ravaisson, and particularly Blondel, who stressed the dynamic aspect (*action*).

Two Polish philosophers have emphatically supported voluntaristic conception. One, Cieskowski, opposed Descartes's "I think, therefore I am" with his "I will, therefore I think and am." The other, W. Lutoslawski, was the author of a book in German, *Seelenmacht*, and one in English, *The World of Souls*.

The Russian Ouspensky in his book *The Fourth Way* underlines the importance of the will and gives instruction for its training. Another important contribution was made by Søren Kierkegaard. Along a similar existential line is Heidegger's concept of the will, which has been ably described by J. Macquarrie in his contribution in *Concepts of Willing*, "Will and Existence."

In sharp contrast to these various voluntaristic conceptions, not only has modern scientific psychology in general abstained from dealing with the will, but a number of psychologists have even denied its existence! This surprising fact can be attributed to various causes. One is the prevalence of a narrow conception of the scientific method, which has been identified with objective *quantitative* techniques (measurements, statistics, etc.) as used in the natural sciences. This has resulted in the will not being considered a subject amenable to scientific investigation. This position has contributed to the widespread acceptance of the strictly deterministic view assumed by behaviorism and Freudian psychoanalysis. Another cause for denying the existence of the will is the reaction to the purely theoretical and often metaphysical conceptions of the will held by philosophers and theologians, and to the consequent endless discussions about "free will." Another is the reaction against the mistaken conception of the will on the part of eighteenth-century moralists and educators, who saw it as a repressive and coercive function systematically opposed and inimical to the natural human drives. And then there is the fact of the close connection existing between the will and the self, or ego. Until recently, scientific psychology has bestowed only limited attention on the study of the self. The will has thus been correspondingly neglected.

The fact that "academic" psychologists have found the subject of the will both intriguing and embarrassing has been expressed with unconscious humor in the following statement in the *Dictionary of Psychological and Psychoanalytic Terms*, by H. B. and A. C. English, a work compiled with praiseworthy precision and objectivity.

> . . . popular psychology has a pretty complete doctrine of *will and voluntary activity*. Scientific psychology has scarcely reached the point where it is possible to define how the terms are to be used. It is probable that a number of quite distinct sets of facts have been brought together under the one term. However, it does not seem possible to dispense with the concept of a class of behaviors, to be called voluntary, that differ from other behaviors in a number of ill-defined ways. Though it is not easy to say how, voluntary movement does seem to be empirically different from involuntary movement.

S. Hiltner has remarked in a more drastic statement, "Though for different reasons both psychology and theology have been occupied with matters which made the concept of the will unnecessary, or even a positive affront . . . the time has come for a reconsideration of whether, as Mark Twain is reported to have said about reports of his own death, the 'demise of the will has been exaggerated.' "

The existing confusion and diversity of opinion concerning the will may be ascribed to several factors. Many have attributed to it too broad and general a meaning, including even an "unconscious will," although a clear awareness and a deliberate choice of an aim, or purpose, to be attained is an essential characteristic of the human will. Then again, several writers have dealt with the subject in a loose and popular way, emphasizing only the "power" of the will, and making exaggerated claims about its wonders. In addition, other writers have used the word "will" when actually referring to other psychological functions. Two examples will illustrate this: P. E. Levy, in his book *L'Éducation rationnelle de la volonté*, limits himself almost entirely to speaking about the technique of suggestion. Duchâtel and Warcollier emphasize only the power of the imagination in *Les Miracles de la volonté*. Dr. W. H. Sheldon's *Psychology and the Promethean Will* consists for the most part of an able exposition of the nature and meaning of *conflict*, but he gives the will only a cursory and incidental mention. On the other hand, some writers have dealt with the will without actually using the word, a case in point being Mathurin's excellent *Self-Knowledge and Self-Discipline*.

While it cannot be said that the will has been totally ignored by modern academic psychologists, it must be pointed out that most of those who have dealt with it have afforded it only partial consideration and have failed to recognize its central importance and position in human psychic life. For example, Wundt is considered a "voluntarist," but his conception of the will is one-sided and limited. He reduces it to a series of emotional processes. Foreseeing of the end to be attained is omitted as unessential.

At different periods of his scientific activity, William James made valuable contributions to the psychology of the will, fully recognizing the reality and importance of the willing function. His *Principles of Psychology* contains an analysis of the various types of decision-making, which emphasizes the motor element, or impulse, of representations, or mental images. He also referred to the "power of voluntary attention" and pointed out the importance of the stage of affirmation, the "fiat," but he formulated no coherent and inclusive concept of the will. Freedom of the will, he concluded, was a mystery, but the "deterministic view can never receive objective proof"; and, he asserted, "I myself hold with the 'free-willists.' " He also declared, "I will go a step further with my will, not only act with it, but believe as well; believe in my individual reality and creative power."

The Swiss psychologist Édouard Claparède recognized that an act, in order to be voluntary, must be intentional and imply a choice and preparation for the future. But he asserted that "every voluntary act is the expression of a conflict and a struggle . . . and the function of the will is precisely to resolve the conflict." This last statement, however, is not consistent with the fact that some voluntary acts are effortless; for instance, those in which the self willingly gives assent to an urge, or drive, which it considers to be justified or good. Moreover, the direction of the execution, which is the last stage of the willed action, does not usually require conflict, being fundamentally the supervision of the activities executed by other psychological functions.

Another Swiss psychologist, Jean Piaget, also maintained that willing always presumes a conflict of tendencies, but his analysis of the process of willing does not include a recognition of its specific nature, which he reduces to an interaction between cognition and affect.

The various proponents of depth psychology hold diverse and divergent views about the will functions. Freud and "orthodox" psychoanalysts ignore or even deny the existence of the will on the basis of their deterministic philosophy. (Determinism should be considered a philosophy because it lacks scientific proof, as William James stated and as developments in modern science are increasingly demonstrating.) Jung, at the end of *Psychological Types*, writes, "I regard as will the sum of psychic energy which is disposable to consciousness. According to this conception, the process of the will would be an energetic process that is released by conscious motivation. A psychic process, therefore, which is conditioned by unconscious motivation I would not include under the concept of the will." However, while he recognized and even emphasized the reality and the dynamic function of goals, aims, and purposes, he did not make an investigation of the various aspects and stages of the will, nor did he include the use of the will in his therapeutic procedures.

Alfred Adler regarded the will chiefly as an unconscious striving to overcome physical and psychological inferiorities, as having a "compensatory function." A French psychologist, Edgar Forti, an independent follower of Adler's "individual psychology," made a detailed study of the connection between Adler's doctrine and practice and the "will psychology," as well as between Adler's views and "characterology," conceived as the investigation and classification of different tendencies and behavior.

Charles Baudoin, who founded and directed for many years the Institut International de Psychagogie et de Psychothérapie in Geneva, made a penetrating analysis of the willing function, according chief importance to the stage of *decision*. It implies, he says, sacrifice and relinquishing, and he points out that the word "decision" is derived from the Latin verb *caedere*, which means "to cut." Beyond this, however, he did not extend his subtle and valuable investigations on the functioning of psychological energy to the development of the concept of the will; nor did he make use of the techniques of willing in his psychotherapeutic work.

Among depth psychologists, Otto Rank accords special prominence to the will-function and has worked out a theoretical system based on it. The complicated nature of his theory precludes a brief description of it here, and moreover Rank changed his views to the extent of adopting contrary standpoints at different times in the course of its elaboration. As Ira Progoff says in his able exposition of Rank's ideas, "He was interested mainly in stressing the degree of freedom that the individual possesses in contrast to the biological determinism implied in Freud's theory of the instincts." "The human being," Rank says, "experiences his individuality in terms of his will, and this means that his personal existence is identical with his capacity to express his will in the world." But Rank, who had been strongly influenced by Nietzsche, made no distinction between instinct, wish, and will, or between the self-assertive, selfish will of the ego and the will "as a primary instrument of creative and religious experience"—the "will to immortality." Moreover, he made a sharp differentiation between his theories on the will and his use of the conscious will as a therapeutic agent, maintaining that the two have to be kept separate.

Side by side with these developments, and mostly antedating them, a certain amount of experimental investigation of the ways in which the will-function operates has been carried out by various researchers. Narciss Ach and Albert Michotte may be regarded as pioneers in this field, followed by Aveling, Bartlett, and some others. These are mentioned by Aveling in *Personality and Will*, in which he summarizes and ably discusses their methods and results. The approach was experimental, based on measurements of reaction time, of a number of electrical parameters of the organism, and of other physiological variables. Many interesting results were observed, among them the importance of attention (thus confirming the intuition of William James) and the distinction between will, conation, and striving. "Between true willing and striving, or carrying out the operation willed, there was a difference in the kind of mental processes. . . . A volition ensuing even in difficult action may be absolutely effortless. Will is not itself effort, though it may initiate effort of an extraordinary kind."

Along with the experiments, both Ach and Aveling made fine introspective analyses of the various phases of the will act. Their descriptions are too long to be reported here; I shall mention only that one of the most important phases described is the experience of an "actual," or "lived," element expressed as "I truly will." According to Ach, "this experience is essential to all voluntary decision . . . when it is not experienced . . . the conscious process is not a voluntary one." Other experimental investigations carried out by Webb and Lankes demonstrate the difference between perseveration, perseverance, and will.

But this promising line of early experimental research has not been actively pursued.* Only in the last few years has the subject of willing attracted the attention of, and been discussed by, some psychologists, psychoanalysts, and other writers.

L. H. Farber has published a thought-provoking and controversial book, *The Ways of the Will.* In it he postulates "two realms of the will": the first is not a matter of experience and is therefore unconscious; the second is experienced as present and consciously goal-directed. While to regard as "will" the unconscious "moving in a certain direction" (first realm) does not seem warranted, Farber's clear and explicit conception of "will as responsible mover" is valuable. Without it, he remarks, "we tend to smuggle will into our psychological systems under other names."

An important contribution on the central position of the will in the human constitution and in psychotherapy has been made by Wolfgang Kretschmer. Following the lead of the psychiatrist Ernst Kretschmer, who, in his investigations of man's various biological constitutions and brain physiology, advocated occupational therapy for mental patients, he asserts that the will is the basis, the "ground," of knowledge, because it, like everything else in man, presupposes and requires energy (*dynamis*) and movement. He regards "archetypes" as basic forms of the will in operation and draws attention to the relationship between knowledge and will. He considers the central task of psychotherapy to be the re-establishing of the union between them, thus creating the synthesis of the personality.

* Recently an important series of researches has been carried on which demonstrate experimentally the action of the will in producing specific electric waves in the brain as well as physiological and psychological effects.

These researches have been conducted chiefly in the United States and Japan. Particular mention should be made of the work done by Elmer E. Green, Director of the Psychophysiological Laboratory of the Menninger Foundation, and his wife, Alyce M. Green. They have summed up their findings in an article, "Voluntary Control of Internal States: Psychological and Physiological," in the *Journal of Transpersonal Psychology*, 1970, no. 1.

In recent years two developments have opened the way for dealing with the subject of the will in a more understanding and fruitful manner. One has been the rapid growth of the existential, humanistic, and transpersonal psychologies. The other is the emergence of a broader and at the same time more refined conception of the scientific method. This new conception has been brought to light through the ideas of general semantics, and, more directly, through the open-minded and original analysis of the scientific method by A. H. Maslow.

In this context, Frankl's concept and practice of logotherapy deserves mention and appreciation. He emphasized the "will-to-meaning" as a fundamental urge and need.

Recently, an important and valuable book on the will has appeared, Rollo May's *Love and Will*. The author clearly recognizes and comments forcefully upon both humanity's present lack of capacity for willing and the urgent necessity for the rediscovery and use of the will. He says, "The inherited basis of our capacity for will and decision has been irrevocably destroyed. And ironically, if not tragically, it is exactly in this portentous age, when power has grown so tremendously and decisions so necessary and fateful, that we find ourselves lacking any new basis for will." In this analysis of the willing function, May ably points out the connections between wish and will, from which emerge some of the essential characteristics of the will. But according to him, the basis, the root of the will, is what he calls and describes as "intentionality." "Intentionality in human experience underlies will and decision. It is not only prior to will and decision but makes them possible." This same recognition has been formulated in Chapter 12 of the present book. Intentionality is an essential part of the first stage of the willing action. It must precede, and makes possible, all the subsequent stages. It is inherent in the goal, purpose, and motivation, and involves evaluation and meaning, which, as we have seen, are all aspects of the first stage of "willing."

An important recognition which Rollo May makes is the

close connection between intentionality and identity. "It is in intentionality and will that the human being experiences his identity. 'I' is the 'I' of 'I can.' . . . What happens in human experience is 'I conceive—I can—I will—I am.' The 'I can' and 'I will' are the essential experience of identity." This is in full agreement with the previously mentioned statements of Cieskowsky and Aveling. Another valuable contribution of Rollo May is his chapter on "The Relation Between Love and Will." "Man's task," he says, "is to unite love and will. They are not united by biological growth but must be part of our conscious development . . . the relating of love and will . . . points towards maturity, integration, wholeness." He also associates will with "commitment" and "care." But on this point a reservation is called for because of the existence of a "selfish will." This might be considered the opposite of "care" and the "communion of consciousness," which, according to May, characterize the higher will. Another point in May's book that calls for some reservation is his great emphasis on the "demonic," which he makes without clearly distinguishing between its various forms. Socrates' *daimon*, for example, is more akin to the Transpersonal Self than to the dark, instinctual, "demonic" forces.

While transpersonal psychology has not yet dealt specifically with the subject of the will, Maslow has made a brief but clear reference to the deliberate use of the will in a transpersonal direction. "In principle, it is possible, through adequate understanding . . . to see *voluntarily* under the aspect of eternity, to see the sacred and symbolic *in* and *through* the individual here-and-now instance."

Psychosynthesis, in which are combined the empirical, existential, humanistic, and transpersonal conceptions and methods, accords to the will a pre-eminent position and regards it as the central element and direct expression of the "I," or self. In keeping with its empirical approach, psychosynthesis directs the main attention not to the "concept" of the will but to the analysis of the "willing action" in its various stages, to the specific aspects and qualities of the will, and to the practical techniques for the development and the optimum use of the will-function.

The considerable amount of investigation and discussion of the will, which this survey cursorily examines, is not incompatible with the previously made statement about the neglect or even the denial of the will by psychologists. The investigations mentioned have been generally ignored by the main stream of modern academic psychology, and in any case have made no impact upon it. They can be said to have formed a more or less independent rivulet which has remained dissociated from the main stream. Two recent books give a vivid picture of the confusion, misconceptions, and clash of opinions that still encompass the subject of the will. In one of them, *The Concept of Willing*, a number of psychologists and theologians have made a serious and commendable attempt to define this concept. While most of the contributions present interesting information and points of view, the book's editor, Dr. James N. Lapsley, honestly admits in his discerning and objective summary (revealingly entitled "The Concept of the Will—Alive?") that "just as there was no consensus about how one gets to the phenomenon of the function of willing, so there was none regarding what one finds when and if one arrives." Pruyser ends his able historical survey in this collection by pointing out the inadequacies in past and present conceptions of the will, and comes to the conclusion that the "problem of the will remains a difficult challenge to psychologists, theologians, philosophers, ethicists, and all others who are interested in willing."

The other book, *Qu'est-ce que c'est vouloir* (*What Is It to Will?*), comprises a series of papers by a group of medical doctors and theologians delivered at a conference held at Bonneval, France, in the psychiatric clinic of Dr. Henry Ey. It presents a variety of divergent, even contradictory, views ranging from Saint Thomas Aquinas's traditional concept of the will to the extreme position held by a psychoanalyst, Dr. S. Leclair, who candidly avows his perplexity about what to do with the concept of the will, constituting as it does a problem "which has not been formulated in the analytical field." He goes so far as to deny the reality of Freud's *libido* as an energy, relegating it to the status of a metaphorical expression: it is little wonder that, in his introductory summary of the various papers, Father L. Beirnaert concedes that they create more problems than they solve. Besides the nine theoretical papers, the book contains two valuable essays on methods of training the will. This is a subject which a number of educators (Payot, Eymieu, Dwelshauvers, etc.) have dealt with.

The most striking conclusion to be drawn from this historical survey is that attempts to solve the problem of the will on theoretical, intellectualistic lines have led not only to no solution but to contradiction, confusion, and bewilderment. This being so, a way out of the impasse needs to be sought in another direction, one that can produce useful and practical results. Such a way exists: its starting point is the *direct, existential experience of willing*, unhampered by preconceived notions; and it proceeds to a description of the data yielded and to the *institution of experiments* on the various stages, characteristics, and uses of the *willing action*.

The present book has been written with the specific purpose of providing signposts pointing in such a direction and presenting a comprehensive program of research and application in the field of this neglected but so important and essential *reality* of human life.

APPENDIX FIVE

DIFFERENTIAL PSYCHOLOGY

According to the *Dictionary of Psychological and Psychoanalytical Terms*, differential psychology is "the branch of psychology that investigates the kinds, amounts, causes and effects of individual or group differences in psychological characteristics."

Though differential psychology can be regarded from several angles, depending upon different points of view and frames of reference, it is possible to distinguish three principal branches:

I. *Traits, or Factor, Psychology*
II. *Typology*
III. *The Psychology of the Individual, or "Idiographic Psychology"*

Traits, or Factor, Psychology

This consists in the analytical examination of the *traits*, or *characteristic elements*, which serve to describe a person's make-up. This descriptive approach, the object of much research, has revealed itself in practice to be inadequate as a procedure for *understanding* a human being. In the first place, the very number of these traits is confusing. Gordon Allport states that English has about eighteen thousand designations for distinctive forms of personal behavior, and that this figure is greatly exceeded when they appear in combination. Moreover, contradictory traits are not infrequently to be met with in the same person. Allport quotes the following case, which clearly illustrates the point:

> Take the case of Dr. D., always neat about his person and desk, punctilious about lecture notes, outlines, and files; his personal possessions are not only in order but carefully kept under lock and key. Dr. D. is also in charge of the departmental library. In this duty he is careless; he leaves the library door unlocked, and books are lost; it does not bother him that dust accumulates. Does this contradiction in behavior mean that Dr. D. lacks personal dispositions? Not at all. He has two opposed stylistic dispositions, one of orderliness and one of disorderliness. Different situations arouse different dispositions. Pursuing the case further, the duality is at least partly explained by the fact that D. has *one* cardinal (motivational) disposition from which these contrasting styles proceed. The outstanding fact about his personality is that he is a self-centered egotist who never acts for other people's interests, but always for his own. This cardinal self-centeredness (for which there is abundant evidence) demands orderliness for himself, but not for others.

Typology

From ancient times up to the present day, various systems for classifying human types have been developed. Their descriptions and a discussion of them would occupy an entire book and, to be of practical value, would have to be followed by the examination of the psychosynthetic methods specific to each type. Here I will limit myself to a rapid enumeration of the principal types. Their multiplicity and diversity are reflected in the different classifications into which they fall, from binary and ternary to larger groupings up to twelve.

In the binary classifications the primary and fundamental dichotomy is between the "masculine" and the "feminine" types. They correspond to the two fundamental aspects of reality, of life, which are termed by the Chinese Yang and Yin, and by the Indians Purusha and Prakriti. In this context, however, I am referring solely to the two *psychological* types, masculine and feminine, and their characteristics and qualities. Some other binary classifications are:

1. Nominalist—Realist
2. Classicist—Romantic
3. Philistine—Bohemian
4. Apollonian—Dionysiac (Nietzsche)
5. Tenderhearted—Tough-minded (James)
6. Empiricist—Rationalist
7. Primary function—Secondary function
8. Active—Reflective (Gross)
9. Schizoid—Cyclothymic (Kretschmer)
10. Inner-directed—Outer-directed
11. Extravert—Intravert

An ancient ternary classification is the Indian one of *Tamas* (*Rajas*)—*Rajas* (Activity)—*Sattva* (Harmony-Rhythm). A modern one that has been widely adopted differentiates between visual, auditory, and kinesthetic (or motor) types. Then there is that advanced by Sheldon: viscerotonic, cerebrotonic, and somatotonic (endomorph, ectomorph, and mesomorph).

The quaternary groupings include the old one based on the four temperaments: sanguine, phlegmatic, choleric, and melancholic; and Jung's classification according to what he considered to be the four psychic functions: sensation, feeling, thought, and intuition. Heymans and Wiersman have developed an eightfold classification, elaborated by René Le Senne, in which emotionality, activity, and primary and secondary functions are combined in various ways. Jung's grouping of the four functions combined with the two psychological types, extravert and intravert, also can be considered an eightfold classification.

There is also a septenary classification: the aesthetic/creative type, the will/power type, the love/illuminative type, the devotional/idealistic type, the scientific/rational type, the organizer/ritualistic type, and the active/practical type.

Finally, there is a twelve-type classification by the Swiss educator Adolphe Ferrière, who has been, along with John Dewey and Maria Montessori, one of the major pioneers in the field of the "new education." He relates his types to the twelve zodiacal types described by astrologers, but quite independently of the validity of astrology per se. Jung and Keyserling have also used astrological symbols in this manner. Ferrière designates his types in the following rather peculiar way: 1. Original, spontaneous; 2. Primitive; 3. Imaginary; 4. Conventional; 5. Individual; 6. Logical; 7. Sociable; 8. Unquiet; 9. Intuitive; 10. Ascetic; 11. Mystical; 12. Accomplished (Fulfilled).

This widespread tendency to classify human types is similar in many respects to the early attempts to classify chemical substances. There were many mistakes, much floundering, and many incompatible and arbitrary classifications of questionable value: our knowledge of chemical substances was not sufficiently deep, and we had not yet learned to distinguish between *superficial* and *fundamental* differences. But eventually this effort led to the discovery of the periodic table and to the classification of the basic elements in about a hundred types of atoms. This brought order out of much confusion in our conception of matter, and gave a forceful impetus to modern chemistry.

A classification is most useful if it helps one to recognize and understand differences of type that *already exist* within the scheme of nature. On the other hand, a classification based on artificial, arbitrary, or superficial divisions will be of limited practical value, and may become an obstacle and a cause of distortion in our perception of reality. So it is important to consider when a classification is appropriate and useful and when it is not. A classification based on naturally existing categories does not in any way negate the basic unity and the common aspects among types. We know today that the many types of atoms are *different*, yet formed by the *same* elementary particles, according to the *same* universal laws. Ice, water, and vapor represent different types of water. Yet we know that they are different types of *appearance*, different states of the *same* substance. Similarly, we recognize many distinct colors—although there can be intermediate shades that bridge the gap between any two colors and there is therefore no separation in principle. And light itself changes color in a continuous, gradual way as it changes its rate of vibration. It is interesting to note that scientists today describe color in terms of a number corresponding to its wave length, thus recognizing that there is no separation. The artist, on the contrary, thinks of colors primarily as specific and distinct entities. But he is free to mix them in any proportion, so this classification is in no way an obstacle to his artistic expression.

In the psychological field, the many existing classifications have been shown to have a widely varying degree of practical usefulness. On the one hand they have given much evidence that there exist in nature groups of qualities, characterizing individuals, that can be recognized and classified according to type, thus yielding a better understanding of human beings. On the other hand, these classifications have clearly shown how divergent are the viewpoints and the criteria associated with them, and how more or less one-sided and incomplete have been, to this time, all the type classifications based on them. Therefore, the tendency—rather, the temptation—to accord an excessive value to typological classifying needs to be resisted; and even more the inclination to attach labels to individuals. Those who are attracted by such "cataloguing" often become harmfully conditioned and limited by it, while others rightly rebel against it. The inadequacies and limitations resulting from rigid and static typological classifying have been plainly indicated and criticized by both Allport and Maslow.

With these reservations, typological descriptions based on

the more fundamental differences, and therefore able to take into the fullest possible account the complexity and fluidity of the psychological life of individuals can, if wisely employed, lend substantial aid to a deeper and more precise understanding. But they call for further refinement and for appropriate consideration of the many psychological dimensions. Most of all, they must be subtle and flexible, open to individual shades and colorings, overlappings and interpenetrations. They should not be simplistic, nor should they pretend to be final, but must allow for the continuing change and unlimited potential for growth of every individual.

An example of such a constructive development is the fundamental typological division between extraverts and intraverts. That predominantly extraverted or intraverted people exist is evident. This distinction can be of help in acquiring a *first* knowledge of an individual, but it is insufficient by itself. When one speaks of an intravert or extravert, one is really referring to a *tendency*, or *direction*, of his life interest, which, as Allport rightly maintains, is a *disposition* of the individual. When this disposition, this orientation of the vital interest, is predominant, the person may be said to be extraverted or intraverted.

As an example of intraversion I will cite Immanuel Kant, the Königsberg philosopher. Focusing his entire interest on the study of the mind, of intellectual consciousness and its laws, he reached the point of never caring to leave his native city. An even more intraverted type was the French novelist Marcel Proust, whose intraversion can be considered to be pathological. Hating daylight and ordinary human activities, he passed a large part of his life in a cork-paneled room, occupied in describing with great subtlety the conscious and unconscious mental processes of the characters of his novels.

Extremely extraverted types are represented by the great men of action, all of them oriented toward the conquest of the external world. We can mention Julius Caesar and Napoleon, and, in the technical sphere, such great inventors as Edison and Marconi.

But a closer consideration reveals that things are not so simple. One meets first an important difference between the *active* and the *passive* character in both extraversion and intraversion. The men of outstanding ability mentioned above were *active* intraverts or extraverts. But there are *passive*—more precisely, reactive—extraverts as well, who present a very different picture. Sensitive and impressionable, their attention is attracted, I would say monopolized, by external influences, to which they are hypersensitive. The passive extravert's marked susceptibility creates in him a tendency to accept other people's points of view and respond to their psychic influences. The hypnotized subject represents an extreme case of passive extraversion. All of us exhibit a temporary state of passive extraversion when reading a newspaper or book, and when watching a film or television.

An excessive interest in one's physical or psychological state is a feature of passive intraversion. It can lead to oversolicitude about one's physical condition, to fear of disease, to hypochondria. The schizophrenic may be described as an extreme intravert. The depressive phase of manic-depressive psychosis is characterized by morbid passive intraversion, in contrast to the manic phase, which exhibits excessive and morbid extraversion.

Leaving the extreme cases, and turning our attention to the great majority of people, we find that the disposition, or tendency, toward extraversion or intraversion is often not greatly marked, and also that these states *alternate* in the same person in response to different conditions. There is first of all the matter of *age*. In the case of the infant in the first months of life, one may speak of a condition of intraversion, in the sense that the baby is entirely absorbed in the sensations of its own body. Then little by little it turns its attention and interest toward the outside world and other beings, thus passing into a phase of increasing extraversion. This culminates in childhood and prepuberty, in which activism, self-assertion, and a rebellious attitude toward others manifest themselves. With the awakening of the new and often conflicting elements of adolescence, the attention veers once more toward the interior; the adolescent is taken up with his feelings, urges, and personal problems. Once the crisis of adolescence is past, the young individual and later on the mature person tend toward extraversion, to self-affirmation in the external world in relation to others, and often against others.

The later years and old age, on the other hand, see a return to intraversion. Interest in the external world and its achievements gradually subsides and is replaced, according to circumstances, either by a withdrawal into egocentricity and preoccupation with physical health, or by a serene, detached view of the world and an interest in spiritual reality and values.

Then, other differences must be taken into consideration. The disposition to extraversion or intraversion combines with other individual variations: one of the most important is the predominance of one or another of the principal psychological functions. As I have previously mentioned, Jung classified these types according to what he considered man's four fundamental functions, thus distinguishing the sensory type, the feeling type, the thinking type, and the intuitive type. When the sensory function predominates, the interest may be directed either toward bodily sensations or toward sensory impressions reaching us from the external world. This disposition was well characterized by the artist who remarked, "I am one for whom the external world *exists.*" When the feeling function is uppermost, the person can be described as living in a world of emotions and feelings, of personal relationships, of attractions or attachments and aversions. The mental, intellectual type is easily recognized and does not call for specific comment. Cases of the intuitive function predominating are less common, but, interestingly, are on the increase.

It is important to realize how profoundly individuals belonging to these various types differ from one another; they may be said to inhabit virtually different worlds, which scarcely come in contact. A simple example will suffice to clarify this fact. Let us imagine that four individuals, each belonging to a different type, are looking at a landscape. The interest of the sensory-practical man will be focused on the areas of the fields before him, their productiveness, and the value of the land. The feeling type may be most aware that the peaceful scene evokes in him a feeling of serenity, of harmony, of calm and softness. If he is an artist, he might give all his attention to the lines and colors, the light and shade, noting the different tones of green, the contrast between the dark patches of the clumps of trees and the delicate tints of the meadows. The aesthetic values of the scene would constitute his main interest and pleasure. The third member of the quartet will be thinking about the natural features of the landscape, such as the climate, the type of vegetation, the interesting geological nature of the ground, and the scientific issues these features might pose. The fourth observer will discern in the scene spreading before him an aspect of the radiant glory of divine manifestation. He will behold creation manifest in nature and surrender himself to an ecstatic joy.

If each of these "observers" were to put his impressions on paper, it is probable that the four versions would contain few words in common. Anyone reading them might scarcely believe they all were descriptions of the same "object."

Comprehension of this fact that human beings living externally side by side are *in reality inhabiting different worlds* has great psychological and educational value. It reveals the true cause of much of the fundamental lack of understanding, bitter criticism, and antagonism that complicates life and creates an incalculable amount of unnecessary suffering.

Another important distinction appears both in extraversion and in intraversion and in various psychological functions. There are many people who cannot be said to possess a single predominating disposition. A person can have two tendencies, *manifesting extroversion at one level and introversion at another*. For instance, he may be extravert at the feeling-emotional level and intravert at the mental level, and vice versa. This is obvious also in the case of human groups. Thus it could be said that Englishmen are in general extraverted at the physical level (practical activity) and intraverted at the emotional-feeling level.

Instances of these contrasting dispositions and tendencies in individual persons can be found among religious figures. Saint Theresa, Saint Catherine of Siena, and Saint Dominic, for example, combined a pronounced mystical intraversion with a practical extraversion which made them "activists," led them to found great organizations and, in the case of Saint Catherine, to exercise a decisive influence on the history of her times. Saint Catherine may thus be classified as an intravert at the emotional and intuitive levels and as an active extravert at the physical level.

Further, there are two other opposite directions followed by the life interest which must be recognized and given adequate consideration. One is "downward," which can be termed *infraversion*, the other "upward," or *supraversion*. In infraversion, the aim is to plumb the unconscious in its lower aspects. This is a major concern of psychoanalysis, and it has been termed "the descent into hell." It may be compared to underwater diving. In supraversion, on the other hand, the life interest and psychological investigation are directed toward the higher aspects of the psyche, i.e., toward the superconscious and the Self. Supraversion is comparable to mountaineering.

What has been said should not be interpreted as undervaluing infraversion and overvaluing supraversion. Here too occur manifestations of different value. There is an infraversion of high quality, the scientific investigation and exploration of the lower unconscious, which might be called psychological geology and archaeology. And excessive supraversion can be used to escape from the problems of life. The psychosynthetic goal is to acquire the ability to direct energies *at will*—that is, through the directing function of the will—in *any* direction and fashion, according to specific purposes, intentions, needs, and demands. This can be called *poliversion*.

Finally, there is a basic difference, or rather contrast, between two directions *in time* of the life interest: between the future-oriented, or *forward-verted*, and the past-oriented, or *retro-verted*. This opposition between progression and regression is going on all the time in each individual, and regression has rightly been pointed out as the cause of many psychological troubles and neurotic symptoms. Collectively, the conflict between those who belong to the two opposite types—the innovator and the revolutionary on one side, and the conservative, clinging to the past, on the other—has reached a level of crucial, acute strife, which pervades the world scene today.

The Unique Individual—Idiographic Psychology

However useful typology may be for understanding and dealing with different human beings, it fails to give a full view, a comprehensive account of an *individual*. Every individual constitutes a unique combination of countless and differing factors. If even the combinations between elements as simple as the lines on the skin of the fingers are so different that fingerprints are sufficient to identify an individual, it is clearly apparent that the combinations of the vast number of biological and psychological characteristics in each single human being make of each of us a most complex, diverse, and genuinely unique individual.

Even more than this, those countless factors and their combinations are not static and fixed as fingerprints are. They are changing constantly, owing both to the inner development and growth of the individual and to the constant impact and intake of influences from the outside world and from other human beings.

But important as this realization is, it should not lead us to believe that it is hopeless to establish a scientific "psychology of the individual."

Such a psychology is possible, and is beginning to be developed. While it takes into due consideration all the contributions we have mentioned up to here, which could be subsumed under the term "descriptive psychology," its chief method is that of *understanding psychology* (*verstehende*, in German). The means for arriving at such understanding or *comprehension from within,* so to speak, has been indicated in different ways, and there is still much confusion in the terminology. Allport made a sophisticated critical survey of the methods indicated by such terms as empathy, sympathy, identification, intuition, acquaintance, participation, and so on. I cannot enter now into a discussion of all of these, but I will try to clarify some basic points. The contrast between "acquaintance with" and "knowledge about" was pointed out, with his usual aptness, by William James, in the following anecdote quoted by Allport. Two Maine fishermen were chatting. They were discussing a college professor who was a summer resident. One said to the other: "He *knows* everything." The other drawled his reply: "Yup, but he don't *realize* nothing." The second fisherman was saying, in effect, that the professor had plenty of knowledge about the world, but had failed to digest it. "William James," says Allport, "like the fisherman, has called attention to the distinction between two kinds of cognition: *knowledge about* and *acquaintance with.* One may know a great deal about Peter, and yet not 'realize' the pattern of his life.

"To be truly acquainted with a person means to be able to take his point of view, to think within his frame of reference, to reason from his premises. Acquaintance leads us to realize that the existence of the other appears rationally consistent from his standpoint, however disjointed it may appear to be from ours."

An analysis of sympathy in its various aspects has been made by Scheler in his book *The Nature of Sympathy,* and is summarized by W. A. Sadler in *Existence and Love.* Sadler also extensively quotes Binswanger, and his conclusion is that this understanding requires union of heart and head, called by Binswanger "loving thinking."

So a holistic, synthetic science of the human being must take into proper account both the basic *common* element existing in all individuals and the differences that make each of them *unique*. This has been so well expressed by Maslow that I shall quote him in full:

> One can even transcend individual differences in a very specific sense. The highest attitude toward individual differences is to be aware of them, to accept them, but also to enjoy them and finally to be profoundly grateful for them as a beautiful instance of the ingenuity of the cosmos—the recognition of their value, and wonder at individual differences. But also, and quite different from this ultimate gratitude for individual differences, is the other attitude of rising above them in the recognition of the essential commonness and mutual belongingness and identification with all kinds of people in ultimate humanness or species-hood, in the sense that everyone is one's brother or sister. Then individual differences and even the differences between the sexes have been transcended in a very particular way. That is, at different times one can be very aware of the differences between individuals; but at another time one can wave aside these individual differences as relatively unimportant for the moment by contrast with the universal humanness and *similarities* between human beings.

Most of what has been said up to this point belongs to the field of so-called "normal" psychology, or (see the diagram on page 14) to the "lower" and "middle" areas (both conscious and unconscious) of the human personality. But there is also the level or realm of the superconscious and of the Transpersonal Self. Here again, and in a more essential sense, we find the paradoxical union or integration and coexistence of the individual and of the universal. This has been discussed in Chapter 10, and put in evidence in the diagrams on page 127.

The Transpersonal Self of each is in intimate union with the Transpersonal Self of all other individuals, however unconscious they may be of this. All Transpersonal Selves can be considered as "points" within the Universal Self. An interesting corroboration of this has been given by the French psychologist Gaston Berger:

> What I have to emphasize is that all our previous analysis "sent us back" constantly to a transcendental subject. All my deductions, which I tried to keep within a positive frame of mind, imply an ending which is not itself included in the series of natural events. I have been talking, for instance, of emotions. But this word means something because it not only evokes some objective modifications, but it points to a consciousness experiencing certain feelings. Relationships which exist among human beings, and about which we have been talking with regard to situations, also point to transcendental subjectivities.
>
> The discovery of the transcendental subject is the conclusive moment of psychological reflection. One can discover transcendental reality through very different ways. Descartes arrives there, and uses his "cogito" in an energetic effort to formulate a proposition about which it would be impossible for him to doubt. Husserl arrives there by what he calls a "phenomenological reduction." "Truth is one, but every philosopher walks towards it by his own path."

Let me close with Berger's penetrating thought:

> Am I now able to answer the question which I was asking at the beginning of my inquiry? Can I say who am I? Nothing could be less sure. I have learned to recognize in the personality more or less profound levels. I have taken back properties to their own principles. But levels cover a center, and properties have an owner. I have pushed as far as possible my investigation without ever being able to get at something more than my belonging. To recognize them as mine, means to differentiate myself from them. I certainly am not either this body through

which sensations come, and which I use for action, nor those tendencies, good or bad ones, that manifest through it. I can even see in the light of experience that *I cannot be* a body or an aggregate of bodies or a characteristic derived from some particular form of bodies. Those hypotheses which I am refusing were not false propositions, but meaningless affirmations. However even if I cannot in any way get hold of myself, I nevertheless *know that I am*, and that I cannot doubt to be. . . . If I wanted to speak more rigorously, I should then say I am I, expressing in this unusual way the fact that the I is always the subject. If I prefer to use a term which belongs both to common use and to the philosopher's language, I will not say, as is sometimes done, that I have a soul (which, to be precise, is contradictory), but that *I am a soul*.

REFERENCE NOTES

Part One: The Nature of the Will

Chapter 2. The Existential Experience of the Will

12. Professor Calò, *Enciclopedia italiana di scienze, lettere ed arti* (Rome, 1929–1939, Vol. 35), p. 559.

Chapter 3. The Qualities of the Will

21. For a more detailed description of effortless volition, and quotations, see Appendix Four, Historical Survey, p. 235, and Francis Aveling, *Personality and Will* (London, 1931), pp. 83ff.
21. A. H. Maslow, *The Farther Reaches of Human Nature* (New York, 1971), p. 68.
23–24. A. H. Maslow, *Motivation and Personality* (New York, 1970), pp. 136–37.
25–26. Ramacharaka, *Raja Yoga* (Bombay, 1966), pp. 125–27.
32. Luigi Fantappiè, *Principi di una teoria unitaria del mondo fisico e biologico* (Rome, 1944).
32. R. Buckminster Fuller, *No More Second Hand God & Other Writings* (Carbondale, Illinois, 1963), p. v.
34. Maslow, *The Farther Reaches of Human Nature*, p. 210.
34. Roberto Assagioli, *Psychosynthesis* (New York, 1971), p. 31.

Chapter 4. The Strong Will

39. William James, *Talks to Teachers* (New York, 1912), pp. 75–76.
39–41. Boyd Barrett, *Strength of Will and How to Develop It* (New York, 1931).

Chapter 5. The Skillful Will: Psychological Laws

50–51. Arnaud Dejardins, *Les Chemins de la sagesse*, Vol. II (Paris, 1971), p. 35.
57. Gustave Le Bon, *La Psychologie de l'éducation* (Paris, 1889).
58. Charles Baudoin, *Suggestion and Autosuggestion* (London, 1922).
64. Roberto Assagioli, *The Transformation and Sublimination of Sexual Energies* (New York, Psychosynthesis Research Foundation, 1963).
65. Frances Wickes, *Inner World of Choice* (New York, 1963), p. 34.

Chapter 6. Practical Applications of the Skillful Will

73. A. H. Maslow, *Motivation and Personality* (New York, 1970), pp. 187–88.
75. The method of neutralization is explained by Patanjali in his *Yoga Sutras*, 33, Book II: "To obstruct thoughts which are inimical to Yoga, contrary thoughts should be brought." (Translation by Vivekanada, Almora, 1915.)
82–83. *The Autobiography of Goethe*, translated by John Oxen (London, 1891), pp. 320–23.

Chapter 7. The Good Will

88–89. On empathy, see Laura Huxley's recipe, "Jump in the other person's place," in *You Are Not the Target* (New York, 1965), pp. 56–60.

Chapter 8. Love and Will

94. Petrim Sorokin, *The Ways and Power of Love* (Boston, 1959).
94. Martin Luther King, *The Strength of Love* (New York, 1963).
96. Among the various writers who have pointed out that love is an art, Erich Fromm has contributed a particularly clear and penetrating study in his book *The Art of Loving* (New York, 1956).

98. A. H. Maslow, *Motivation and Personality* (New York, 1970), p. 21.

103. Hermann Keyserling, *The Recovery of Truth* (New York, 1929), p. 103.

104. Roberto Assagioli, "The Balance and Synthesis of the Opposites" (New York, Psychosynthesis Research Foundation, 1972).

Chapter 9. The Transpersonal Will

106. This sense of dissatisfaction has been briefly described in *Psychosynthesis*, p. 41.

107. *Ever more . . . "abyss-experience"*: Viktor E. Frankl, *The Will to Meaning* (New York, 1969), p. 83.

107. *"The existential vacuum . . . it"*: ibid., p. 86.

107–109. Leo Tolstoi, *A Confession* (London, 1940), pp. 15–19.

111. C. G. Jung, *Modern Man in Search of a Soul* (New York, 1933), p. 32.

112. *The most . . . vision*: Daisetz Taitaro Suzuki, *Essays in Zen Buddhism* (New York, 1949), p. 126.

112. *The Man . . . live*: quoted by Viktor Frankl, *op. cit.*, p. 50.

114. R. M. Bucke, *Cosmic Consciousness* (New York, 1951).

114. William James, *The Varieties of Religious Experience* (New York, 1902).

114. Winslow Hall, *Observed Illuminates* (London, 1926).

114–15. Francis Thompson, in *Immortal Poems of the English Language* (New York, 1960), p. 476.

115. C. G. Jung, *The Integration of the Personality* (London, 1940), pp. 291–96.

119. A. H. Maslow, "Theory Z," *Journal of Transpersonal Psychology*, I:2, pp. 31–47. Reprinted in A. Maslow, *The Farther Reaches of Human Nature* (New York, 1971), pp. 280–95.

120. F. Haronian, "Repression of the Sublime," in James Fadiman (ed.), *The Proper Study of Man* (New York, 1971), p. 240; reprinted by Psychosynthesis Research Foundation, New York, 1972.

120. *In my . . . fate*: quoted by Haronian and reprinted in Maslow, *op. cit.*, p. 35.

120–21. *Transcendence . . . nature*: *op. cit.*, pp. 274–75.

Chapter 10. The Universal Will

128. Lama Anagarika Govinda, *The Way of the White Clouds* (Berkeley, 1970), pp. 124–25.

128. Sarvepalli Radhakrishnan, "Human Personality," in Clark Moustakas, ed., *The Self* (New York, 1956), p. 118.

129. A. H. Maslow, *The Farther Reaches of Human Nature* (New York, 1971), p. 277.

130–31. The quotation from Dante is adapted from the translation by Geoffrey Bickersteth (Cambridge, England, 1932).

Part Two: The Stages of Willing

Chapter 12. Purpose, Evaluation, Motivation, Intention

145–46. Pierre Teilhard de Chardin, in *The Phenomenon of Man* (New York, 1964), has given some inspiring ideas on the future of the psychospiritual evolution, based on past and present biophysic development.

Chapter 13. Deliberation, Choice, and Decision

152–53. Professor Calò, from his article on the will in *Enciclopedia italiana di scienze, lettere ed arti,* Vol. 35 (Rome, 1929–1939), p. 17.

Chapter 14. Affirmation

171. Hermann Keyserling, *From Suffering to Fulfilment* (London, 1938), pp. 111, 184–85.

Chapter 15. Planning and Programing

185. For correct handling of the psychological phases of elaboration of gestation, see my paper "Modes and Rhythms of Psychological Formation" (in Italian) (Florence, Italy, Istituto Psicosintesi, 1968).

Chapter 16. The Direction and the Execution

195. Robert Desoille, "The Guided Daydream" (New York, Psychosynthesis Research Foundation, 1966).

195. Leuner, *American Journal of Psychotherapy*, 32: 1, 1969, pp. 4–22.

Part Three: Epilogue

Chapter 17. The Joyous Will

200. *Why not . . . happiness*: A. H. Maslow, *The Farther Reaches of Human Nature* (New York, 1971), p. 176.

200. *Levels of needs*: A. H. Maslow, *Toward a Psychology of Being* (New York, 1962), p. 83.

201–202. Evelyn Underhill, *Mysticism* (New York, 1961), p. 437.

Appendices

Appendix Two. Thinking and Meditation

219–20. Swami Vivekanada, *The Complete Works of Vivekanada*, Mayavatl Memorial Edition (Almora, 1915).

Appendix Four. Historical Survey

235. Other views, omitted from the introductory survey in Appendix Four, may be found in the clear "Selective Historical Survey" by Paul W. Pruyser contained in *The Concept of Willing*, edited by J. N. Lapsley (Nashville, Tenn., 1967). The exposition of Kierkegaard's profound views on the will is particularly valuable.

236. *. . . the most important . . . zen appeals to it*: Daisetz Taitaro Suzuki, *Essays in Zen Buddhism* (New York, 1949), pp. 107, 115.

237. W. Lutoslawski, *Seelenmacht* (Leipzig, 1899).

237. W. Lutoslawski, *The World of Souls* (London, 1924).

237. P. D. Ouspensky, *The Fourth Way* (London, 1959).

237. J. Macquarrie, "Will and Existence," in Lapsley, *op. cit.*, pp. 41ff.

238. H. B. and A. C. English, *Dictionary of Psychological and Psychoanalytic Terms* (New York, 1958), p. 587.

238. S. Hiltner, in Lapsley, *op. cit.*, p. 18.

239. P. E. Levy, *The Rational Education of the Will* (London, 1918).

239. Edmond Duchâtel and René Warcollier, *Les Miracles de la volonté* (Paris, 1914).

239. W. H. Sheldon, *Psychology and the Promethean Will* (New York, 1936).

239. Mathurin, *Self-knowledge and Self-discipline* (Aberdeen, 1926).

239. A good exposition and discussion of Wundt's ideas has been made by Francis Aveling in *Personality and Will* (London, 1931), pp. 70–78.

239. William James, *Principles of Psychology* (New York, 1950), pp. 524–25.

239–40. Quotations from William James from *Talks to Teachers* (New York, 1912), pp. 189, 191.

240. C. G. Jung, *Psychological Types* (New York, 1933), pp. 616–17.

241. Edgar Forti, *L'émotion, la volonté et le courage* (Paris, 1952).

241. *"He was . . . instincts"*: Ira Progoff, *The Death and Rebirth of Psychology* (New York), p. 210.

242. *"will to immortality"*: ibid., p. 261.

242. Narciss Ach, *Über die Willenstätigkeit und das Denken* (Gottingen, 1905).

242. Albert Michotte, *Etude experimental sur le choix volontaire* (Louvain, 1910).

242. *"Between . . . kind"*: Francis Aveling, *Personality and Will* (London, 1931), pp. 91, 93.

242. *this . . . one*: ibid., p. 87.

242. *Other experimental . . . will*: ibid., p. 101 (Webb, "Character and Intelligence," *British Journal of Psychology*, Monograph, 1915, and Lankes, "Perseveration," *British Journal of Psychology*, Monograph, 1915.)

243. L. H. Farber, *The Ways of the Will* (New York, 1966).

243. *"archetypes"*: Wolfgang Kretschmer, *Selbsterkenntnis und Willensbildung im ärztlichen Raume* (Stuttgart, 1958), p. 66.

244. *general semantics*: a clear exposition can be found in W. Johnson's *People in Quandaries* (New York, 1946).

244. A. H. Maslow, *Psychology of Science* (New York, 1966).

244. Victor Frankl, *The Will to Meaning* (New York, 1969).

244–45. Rollo May, *Love and Will* (New York, 1969), pp. 182, 223, 201, 243, 283, 286.

245. A. H. Maslow, *Religions, Values, and Peak-Experiences* (New York, 1970).

246. James N. Lapsley, ed., *The Concept of Willing* (Nashville, Tenn., 1967), pp. 55, 50.

246. Henry Ey, *Qu'est ce que c'est vouloir* (Paris, 1958).

Appendix Five. Differential Psychology

248. H. B. and A. C. English, *Dictionary of Psychological and Psycho-analytic Terms* (New York, 1958), p. 152.

248. *the object of much research*: Anne Anastasi, *Differential Psychology* (New York, 1958).

248–49. *contradictory traits*: Gordon Allport, *Pattern and Growth in Personality* (New York, 1961), pp. 353–55.

249. *Take the . . . others*: *ibid.*, p. 363.

250. On Heymans *et al.*, see Gaston Berger, *Caractère et personalité* (Paris, 1962), pp. 13 *et seq.*

251. Adolphe Ferrière, *Vers une classification naturelle des types psychologique* (Nice, 1943).

259. G. Allport, *Pattern and Growth in Personality* (New York, 1961).

259. W. A. Sadler, *Existence and Love* (New York, 1969).

260. A. H. Maslow, "Various Meanings of Transcendence," *Journal of Transpersonal Psychology*, 1:1, reprinted in Maslow, *The Farther Reaches of Human Nature*, p. 278.

261. *What . . . subjectivities*: Gaston Berger, *Caractère et personalité* (Paris, 1962), p. 106.

261. *Truth . . . path*: *ibid.*, p. 105.

261–62. *Am I . . . a soul*: *ibid.*, p. 108. The term "belonging" has been used by Husserl to designate what seems to the subject such an immediate property that it seems to be one thing with the subject himself. See Edmund Husserl, *Méditations Cartésiennes* (The Hague, 1960), and Gaston Berger, *Le Cognito dans la philosophie de Husserl* (Paris, 1941).

INDEX

Gross, O., 250
Guided affective imagery (Leuner), 195
Guided daydream (Desoille), 195

Habits, 57–58
Hall, Winslow, 114
Happiness, 199–200
Harmonization, 44, 86, 121, 130. *See also* Cooperation
Haronian, Frank, ix, 120
Hartmann, Eduard von, 236
Hate, 221–22
Hedonism, 167
Heidegger, Martin, 237
Hemingway, Ernest, 31
Hetzel, 29
Heymans, 250
Hibbert Journal, 34
"Hierarchy of needs." *See* Needs
Hiltner, S., 238
Hitler, Adolf, 16, 174
"Hound of Heaven" (Thompson), 114–15
Humanitarianism, 94, 122, 156, 200
Husserl, Edmund, 261

"I." *See* Self
"I" consciousness. *See* Self-consciousness
Idealism, 144, 155, 180
Ideal model, 37n, 83, 99, 173, 195, 228
Ideals, 94, 140
Ideas, 10, 12, 27, 51–58, 63, 76–77, 80, 94, 229
Idées-forces, 76
Identification, 55, 77, 188, 213–17, 229. *See also* Disidentification; Self-identification
Identity. *See* Self-identification
Idiographic psychology. *See* Psychology, idiographic
Illumination, 111–14, 156, 225–26
Images, 27, 51–57, 67–68, 76–77, 80–81, 194, 206; as technique, 173, 175
Imagination, 46, 49, 53, 66, 83–84, 99, 118, 138–39, 155, 186, 194, 206, 229
Impressions, 54, 227
Impulses, 4, 9, 49, 59, 63, 139, 143, 156, 166–67, 206
Impulsiveness, 164, 166
Indecision, 164–66, 170
Independence. *See* Liberty

Individuality, 33n, 113, 128, 164–166, 188. *See also* Psychology, idiographic
Individuation, 33n
Inertia, 10, 98
Inferiority complex, 165
Infraversion, 257
Inhibitions, 22–23, 46, 60, 84, 152–153, 157, 164
Initiative, 19–20, 28, 31, 205, 230, 233
Inner powers. *See* Powers, inner
Inner presence. *See* Presence, inner
Insight, 30
Inspiration, 156–58, 224, 227
Institut International de Psychopédagogie et de Psychothérapie, 241
Istituto di Psicosintesi, ix, 204
Integration, 19, 31–34, 205, 230, 233
Intellect, 58
Intensity, 19–22, 35, 188, 193–94, 205, 230, 233
Intention, 64–65, 88, 90, 135, 138, 140–41, 144, 154, 163, 183, 205, 230, 232, 233, 244–45
Interaction, psychological, with physical facts, 58–59
Interest, 56, 67; withdrawal of, 57, 75
Interpretation, 157, 223
Interiorization, 64–65
Intraverts, 165, 250, 253–56
Intuition, 49, 124, 139, 156–58, 195–96, 206, 224–26, 255
Invocation, 206

James, William, 25, 39, 51, 58, 114, 239–40, 242, 250, 259
"Jonah Complex," 120
Journal of Transpersonal Psychology, 17
Joy, 9, 24, 37, 40, 64, 75–76, 110, 199–202
Jung, Carl, 33n, 111, 114–15, 124, 240, 250–51, 255

Kant, Immanuel, 124, 253
Keyserling, Hermann, 30, 103, 171, 251
Kierkegaard, Søren, 237
King, Martin Luther, 94, 122
Koans, 223
Kretschmer, Ernst, 243, 250
Kretschmer, Wolfgang, 243
Krishna, 230
Kull, Steven, ix

130; for meaning, 112; trans-
personal (meta-), 106
Neuroticism, 111, 258
Neutralization, 75
Nietzsche, Friedrich Wilhelm, 236,
242, 250
Nightingale, Florence, 122

Observation, 25–26, 192, 194
Observed Illuminates (Hall), 114
Obstacles, 6, 86
Obstinacy, 166
One-Pointedness, 19, 24–27, 205,
230, 233
Organization, 19, 31–34, 205, 230,
233
Origin of Species (Darwin), 29
Ouspensky, P. D., 237

Palombi, Ida, ix
Parapsychology, 162
Patanjali, 75, 235–36
Pathos, 104
Patience, 19, 29–31, 44, 185, 205,
230, 232, 233
Paul, Saint, 171
Peace, 203–204
Peak experiences, 17
Persistence, 5, 11, 19–20, 29–31, 37,
39, 185, 205, 221, 230, 232, 233
Personality, 212, 213, 223, 228;
sub-, 175. *See also* Individuality
Personality and Will (Aveling), 242
Personalization, 33n. *See also*
Individuality
Physical attitudes, 173
Piaget, Jean, 240
Pilot project, 182–83
Planning, 20n, 190; and program-
ing, 33, 135–37, 139, 178–88,
206, 230, 233
Plato, 124, 161
Poisons, psychological, 70–75
Polarity, 104, 129, 186
Poliversion, 257
Power, 10, 46–47, 99, 171, 201;
dynamic, 19–22, 205, 230, 233;
inner, 4–6, 9, 38. *See also* Will,
power
Prajna, 128
Preference, 167–68
Presence, inner, 101
Principles of Psychology (James), 239
Problems, 151–69
Progoff, Ira, 162, 241
Programing. *See* Planning

Project-making, 182–83
Promptings, 157–58
Promptness, 19, 27–28, 205, 230,
233
Proust, Marcel, 253
Pruyser, 246
Psychic atmosphere, 157
Psychic sensitivity, 157
Psychoanalysis, 50, 55, 60, 141, 144,
176, 237, 240, 257
"Psychoanalysis and Psychosynthe-
sis" (Assagioli), 34
Psychological breathing and feed-
ing, 57, 69–78
Psychological elements, 48–49
Psychological energies, 61, 63, 65,
78, 85, 149, 172, 225
Psychological environment, 50,
69–70
Psychological formations, 56–57
Psychological functions. *See*
Functions
Psychological laws. *See* Laws
Psychological types. *See* Types
Psychological Types (Jung), 240
Psychologie de l'education, La (Le
Bon), 57
Psychology: descriptive, 259; differential, 88, 248–62; humanistic,
viii, 88; idiographic, 258–62;
transpersonal, viii, 17, 106; understanding, 259
Psychology and the Promethean (Sheldon), 239
Psychosynthesis, viii, 17, 30, 66, 70,
100, 115, 152, 158, 188, 190, 218,
245–46, 257; educational, 232;
group, 186; individual, 70, 178,
185–86, 232; interpersonal, 178,
186; personal, viii, 33, 121, 137,
206, 223; social, 178, 186; transpersonal (spiritual), 104, 121,
185, 206
Psychosynthesis (Assagioli), viii, 12,
34, 37n, 48n, 64, 84n, 87, 105,
115, 124, 185, 192, 195, 222,
228, 232
Psychosynthesis Institute, 204
Psychosynthesis Research Foundation, 78n
Psychotherapy, 206, 232, 243
"Pull," 113–14, 149
Purification, 64
Purpose, 20n, 29, 33, 52, 135, 138,
140–41, 145, 149, 155, 171, 180,
184, 205, 230, 233, 244